Let's Find The BIG IDEA

Bernice Wells Carlson

Illustrated by Bettye Beach

ABINGDON
Nashville

LET'S FIND THE BIG IDEA

Library of Congress Cataloging in Publication Data

Carlson, Bernice Wells.
  Let's find the big idea.
  Includes index.
  Summary: A collection of nineteen skits and plays based on traditional fables and stories containing universal truths.
  1. Children's plays, American. 2. Fables—Juvenile drama. [1. Plays. 2. Fables—Drama] I. Title
PS3553.A7318L4   812'.54   81-19121   AACR2
                ISBN 0-687-21430-0

"Anyone Could, But—" is reprinted from *Act It Out* by Bernice Wells Carlson, copyright © 1956 by Pierce and Washabaugh (Abingdon Press); "Who's Stronger?" is from *The Right Play for You* by Bernice Wells Carlson, copyright © 1960 by Abingdon Press.

Dedicated to

Carl

and also in memory of my parents
Bernice and George B. Wells
who laid the foundation of this book

Acknowledgments

I must express gratitude to the storytellers of the world, not only to the renowned Aesop, Fontaine, and Perrin whose fables are among those dramatized in this book, but also to the people who down through the ages told and retold fables, often changing them in detail, but not in essence, to make them vital to listeners.

For example: "The Country Mouse and the City Mouse" appears in nineteenth-century readers as a Norse tale and is also found in collections of Aesop's fables. In like manner "The Bundle of Sticks," on which the skit "Together or Alone" is based, is accredited to Aesop and is also found, with some variations, as a Chinese fable.

"The Heart of a Monkey" is a tale from Zanzibar. The same plot with a monkey and a crocodile appears as a tale from India. With a rabbit and a turtle who wants the live eye of a rabbit, it is a fable from Korea. In most cases sources of skits and plays are not given because they are indefinite.

A few plays in this book have definite sources other than those considered traditional: "Problems! Problems!" is based on "The Ragged Pedlar" by Gertrude Landa; "The Law of the Jungle" is based on "Jan, the Animal Judge" by A. C. Stafford; "The Tiger, the Brahman, and the Jackal" is based on a story by Joseph Jacobs; and "Half of the Reward" is based on "The Peasant and the Precious Stone" by Leo Tolstoy.

I wish to thank the many girls and boys who have acted out fables with me in Brownie, Cub and Girl Scouts, in public school classes, in church groups, at camp, and other places.

A special thank you to teachers, librarians, and other friends who helped develop this book: Marie Wilt, retired elementary school-teacher, Cranford, N.J.; Leila Cayce, New Brunswick, N.J. Public Library; Pat Bacon and Christine Wallace, Franklin Township Public Library, Somerset, N.J.; Christine Umberger, Springfield, Va.; Helen Cooke, Bellevue, Wash.; Carol Carlson, Hopewell, N.J.; and Carl Carlson, Somerset, N.J.

Contents

Introduction

Fables are fun to read or act out because they ridicule the foolish things people often say or think and the silly things they do. But fables, short or long and from many countries, are more than jokes. Each one contains a big idea—a concept that can help people understand each other and live together. One definition of a fable is a story to enforce a universal truth.

No one knows who first told fables but some scholars believe that they may have originated among the Jewish and other Semitic peoples and spread through India and the rest of the world. Some fables remained for centuries in the culture of their origin. Those fables of central Africa are unique as are those of other peoples who remained isolated.

The most famous fables are those first told by Aesop, a Greek slave who was engaged to teach Roman boys more than two thousand years ago. Aesop's method was to tell the story, and then point out in a single sentence the meaning of the tale.

The big ideas in Aesop's fables, and those used by many other famous storytellers, are just as true today as they were when first told. Very often, however, the message may need explaining. For example, Aesop said: "Thy pride is but a prologue of thy shame."

"He who compasses the destruction of his neighbor is caught in his own snare."

"If you must revile your neighbor, make certain that he cannot reach you."

How would people say that today? Listeners can decide, sometimes with a little help. Other adages attributed to Aesop are easy to understand, but the words often sound as if they apply only to people who lived long ago and far away.

In using this book, the storyteller asks the audience to listen to a skit or play and discover the meaning. The players act out the fable. The storyteller then asks the listeners, "What is the big idea?"

It may be necessary to coax the audience and urge members to think and speak up. Every answer related to the play is accepted as correct. Some of the plays in this book contain more than one big idea. After a reasonable answer period, the storyteller closes the program by giving one more moral—the one printed at the end of the skit or play. There is no suggeston that this printed moral is the correct one or by any means the best one given.

There are many ways to use this book. Pretend that your fists are puppets. Clench them and say to a younger child, "This is a lion. This is a cub." Act out a skit, renaming the fists as you go along. Or you can cover your hands with large handkerchiefs and do the same.

Make simple puppets and put on a skit for other members of your family or for your neighborhood friends, classmates, members of your Brownie or Cub Scout troop, or any other group. Or you may wish to put on a play without puppets.

Plan a program including music and one or two skits or playlets, or a program combining skits and playlets. This type of program gives a number of people a chance to act.

Produce a longer play. There is room for dramatic activity in every kind of recreation and school-teaching program: church school, day, or residential camps, and various kinds of clubs.

Some of the plays in this book are well-suited for either puppets or live actors. Some are easier to produce as puppet plays, and others require live actors who can move about the stage freely and express emotions with facial expressions and gestures.

Many of the characters in fables are animals who take on human characteristics. If you are portraying an animal, don't wear a mask that covers the face! Words must come out loud and clear.

Don't make elaborate costumes for a simple skit or play. Identify animals by the way they stand or walk, or by having them wear signs with names of characters printed on them. If you want animal costumes, make simple caps with appropriate ears attached and pin tails to jeans or leotards.

The humans in the skits and plays do not need period-piece costumes. A crown suggests a king. A long skirt and apron suggests a peasant woman.

Characters in several of the skits and plays in this book can be played by either girls or boys by changing names. In "Anyone Could, But—" the king may speak to his queen, not the Lord Chamberlain. The queen, not the king, might have someone place the stone in the road and then talk to her lady-in-waiting. Sandy, the lead character, can be either a boy or a girl.

It is better to change a name in a play than to have a girl play a man's part, or vice-versa—unless there is an all-female or all-male cast.

You can put on a skit or play almost any place: in your family room or backyard, in a classroom, under a tree at camp, or on a regular stage. In all cases, keep scenery simple. It is not necessary to spend a lot of time or money creating a realistic setting for a short play, even when you are using a stage with a curtain.

If you are using puppets, you don't need a stage. Hold the puppets in front of you and speak for them. Or stand behind a high-backed chair and make the puppets act above it. You may wish to stretch a sheet across part of a room. Stand behind that and become a puppeteer.

Or if you have a puppet stage you can make use of it. If you want to use a puppet stage and you do not have one, make one. Always remember: Your voice must come out loud and clear. Don't bend over in such a way that you can't use your diaphragm. Your stage voice may sound like yelling, but it's necessary when you have a barrier between you and the audience who must be able to understand every word in order to catch the big idea of the fable.

After you have produced several skits and plays in this book, read more fables and dramatize them yourself. Whether you use material in this book or your own dramatizations, let the big idea in each fable become your own, something to remember and live by.

Skits

A skit is a short dramatic sketch that usually pokes fun at silly attitudes and foolish acting. The characters are types of people, or animals who act like people, not finely developed individuals.

The action in a skit covers a very short time, usually minutes, so the characters must exaggerate what they say and do in order to get the idea across to the audience.

Skits based on fables contain universal truths. Therefore, when producing a skit you should first read it carefully and pick out the lines that give the big idea. Every actor must be ready for these lines.

The person who says the lines must memorize them carefully and be able to deliver them emphatically so that everyone in the audience can hear and understand each word. Other actors must listen to these punch lines and react accordingly.

A few hints to help you get important lines across:

Never wear a mask that covers the face.

Stand as close to the audience as possible.

Face the audience directly.

Speak loudly, slowly, clearly, and with emphasis on key words.

Work as a team—each player reacting to key speeches and action.

A Pearl
in the Barnyard

Characters

COCK	OTHER HENS
FIRST HEN	CHICKS

SCENE. *A barnyard. Cock is crowing and strut-ting. One hen, or as many hens and chicks as you wish, are listening to him.*

COCK: Cock-a-doodle doo! I found a pearl. Cock-a-doodle doo! I found a pearl. Cock-a-doodle doo! I found a pearl. Cock-a-doodle doo! I found a pearl.

FIRST HEN: You found a pearl. So what?

COCK: So I am the only fowl in the barnyard who has a pearl. Cock-a-doodle doo!

FIRST HEN: All right. You're the only fowl in the barnyard who has a pearl. So what?

COCK: What do you mean? So what?

FIRST HEN: What are you going to do with a pearl?

COCK: Well, I hadn't thought about that.

FIRST HEN: Can you eat a pearl?

COCK: No, I can't eat a pearl.

FIRST HEN: Can you wear a pearl?

COCK: No, I can't wear a pearl.

FIRST HEN: Do you want to sit on a pearl?

COCK (*yelling*): No! I don't want to sit on a pearl.

FIRST HEN: So what are you going to do with a pearl? (*pauses; other characters shake their heads*) Give me corn! I'd rather eat corn than peck on a pearl.

(*Other Hens and Chicks make a racket saying, "Cluck-Cluck! Give me corn," or, "Peep-peep! Give me corn." Cock hangs his head and exits.*)

STORYTELLER: What's the big idea?

Think before you crow.

Belling the Cat

Characters

CAT	MIDDLE MOUSE
CAPTURED MOUSE	SMALLEST MOUSE
BIGGEST MOUSE	OTHER MICE

SCENE. *A home. Mice are chasing each other, cuffing each other, playing in a good-natured way. Cat creeps in, catches one mouse, and drags him away.*

16

CAPTURED MOUSE: Eeek! Eeek! Eeek! (*continues cry until offstage*)

BIGGEST MOUSE: That does it! We must do something about that cat.

MIDDLE MOUSE: Yes, but what?

BIGGEST MOUSE: We'll have a council meeting and discuss the situation.

(*Other mice nod heads and form a semicircle with Smallest Mouse and Biggest Mouse in the center.*)

BIGGEST MOUSE: Now, do you have any ideas?

(*Mice begin to say, "Well—" "I think—" and other appropriate remarks. They gesture as they talk. After a few seconds, Smallest Mouse speaks up.*)

SMALLEST MOUSE: Sir, I have an idea.

BIGGEST MOUSE (*to other mice*): Quiet! (*to Smallest Mouse*) Speak up.

SMALLEST MOUSE: I think we should tie a bell on the cat. Then we could tell when she is coming.

OTHER MICE: Good idea! Splendid! (*and other appropriate remarks*)

BIGGEST MOUSE: Yes, a splendid idea. But who is going to tie the bell on the cat?

OTHER MICE: Not me. Not me. Not me.

STORYTELLER: What's the big idea?

It's easier to suggest an idea than to carry it out.

Think Twice

Characters

SANSUKE, a kitchen maid
JIRO, a gardner   MRS. KAKITO

SCENE. *The garden of a home in old Japan. Sansuke pantomimes picking pole beans. Jiro stands a few feet away hoeing. Sansuke stops and turns toward Jiro.*

SANSUKE: Jiro, I've been thinking.

(*Jiro stops work and turns toward her.*)

JIRO: About what?

SANSUKE: Which is more important, the sun or the moon?

(*Jiro laughs until he can hardly stand up straight.*)

JIRO: Ho-ho-ho! Ho-ho-ho! What a silly *question!* What a *silly* question. Everyone knows the answer. What do you think?

SANSUKE: I think the sun is more important than the moon. The sun is bigger.

JIRO: The sun! Oh, you foolish, foolish woman! You say the sun is more important because it is bigger. Everyone knows that the moon is more important. (*laughs and laughs and laughs*)

SKITS

(Enter Mrs. Kakito. Sansuke and Jiro bow from waist.)

SANSUKE AND JIRO: Good morning, Mrs. Kakito.

MRS. KAKITO: Good morning, Sansuke. Good morning, Jiro. Tell me, Jiro, why are you laughing so hard? What's so funny?

JIRO: Oh, you'll never believe it. Silly Sansuke asks a foolish question and gives a foolish answer. *(laughs hard again)*

MRS. KAKITO: What is the foolish question, Sansuke?

SANSUKE: Which is more important, the sun or the moon? I say the sun.

MRS. KAKITO: What is your answer, Jiro?

JIRO: The moon, of course! Everyone knows that the moon is more important than the sun.

MRS. KAKITO: Why, in your opinion, is the moon more important than the sun?

JIRO: Because the sun shines in broad daylight. The moon shines when it's dark. So the moon is more important than the sun.

MRS. KAKITO *(laughing)*: Oh, Jiro! Jiro! Think again. Why do we have broad daylight? Where does the light come from?

JIRO: Well—

MRS. KAKITO: Think again, Jiro. Think twice before you call anyone else a silly person. *(exits laughing)*

19

STORYTELLER: What's the big idea?

When you cry "fool," the fool may be you.

The Whole Truth

Characters

KING LION	DEER
MRS. LION	FOX
SHEEP	

SCENE. *Land of the beasts. King Lion stands center stage. Mrs. Lion enters. (Use fist puppets with heads that can be removed. The heads of Sheep and Deer are not fastened to the bodies of the puppets, but sit on the top of covered fingers.)*

MRS. LION: Good morning, my husband, King of the Beasts.

KING LION: Ah, what a loving wife! Come here and kiss me.

(*Mrs. Lion hesitates. King Lion speaks louder.*)

KING LION: I said, "Come here and kiss me!"

(*Mrs. Lion inches toward him.*)

KING LION (*roaring*): Kiss me!

(*King Lion lunges toward her and kisses her. She*

doesn't try to push him off, but fans herself with one paw when he has finished.)

KING LION: Now, tell me. Why didn't you want to kiss me?

MRS. LION: I hate to tell you.

KING LION (*roaring*): Tell me!

MRS. LION: I can't. It's too personal.

KING LION: Tell me, or I'll bite off your head!

MRS. LION: Well, I suppose you ought to know. You have bad breath.

KING LION: What? Bad breath? (*Mrs. Lion hurries offstage.*)

That's right! Run away or I'll bite off your head. (*thinks*) Bad breath? Maybe I need a second opinion. (*calls loudly*) Sheep! Sheep! I, Lion, King of the Beasts command you to come here!

SHEEP: Good morning, your Majesty.

KING LION: Good morning, Sheep. I want to ask you a question. Do I have bad breath?

SHEEP: Do you want the truth, the whole truth, and nothing but the truth?

KING LION: Of course, I want an honest answer.

SHEEP: Sir, you do have bad breath. It stinks!

KING LION: What? My breath stinks? Off with your head!

(*King Lion lunges at Sheep. Sheep's head falls off.*)

KING LION: Well! I guess I need a third opinion.

Deer! Deer! I, Lion, King of the Beasts, command you to come here!

(*Deer enters meekly. Looks at Sheep's head.*)

DEER: Good morning, King Lion.

KING LION: Good morning, Deer. I want your honest opinion. Do I have bad breath?

(*Deer looks again at head of Sheep.*)

DEER: Oh, no, your Majesty, King of the Beasts. You do not have bad breath. Your breath is as sweet as the flowers that bloom in the spring, as sweet as—

KING LION (*interrupting*): Liar! Off with your head!

(*King Lion lunges at Deer whose head falls off.*)

KING LION: Deer tried to flatter me. I guess I need a fourth opinion. Fox! Fox! I, Lion, King of the Beasts command you to come here!

(*Fox enters. He looks at head of Sheep and head of Deer and then at King Lion. At last he speaks.*)

FOX: Good morning, your Majesty.

KING LION: Good morning, Fox. I have a question. Do I have bad breath?

(*Fox begins to sniffle and looks again at heads of Sheep and Deer.*)

FOX: I'm sorry, sir. I have a bad cold. I can hardly hear you. Will you repeat the question?

KING LION (*roaring*): Do I have bad breath? Tell me!

FOX: I can't tell you.

KING LION: Can't tell me? Why?

FOX: I have a cold. My nose is stuffed. I can't smell anything. I must go home and go to bed. Good-bye, your Majesty.

(*Fox exits with his head still on his shoulders.*)

KING LION: Grrrrrrrrrrrrrrrrrr!

STORYTELLER: What's the big idea?

If you can't say something nice, change the subject.

Together or Alone?

Characters

FARMER, father or mother in a family
CHILDREN, five, six, or seven of them

SCENE. *A family farm, more than a hundred years ago. Long benches are placed center front, at an angle, with a small space between the ends. There must be room for each child to sit at the correct time and for Farmer to stand between the two ends.*

As the scene opens, children are quarreling,

gesturing wildly. Farmer stands between the ends of the benches. He is adding another piece of twine to a bundle containing as many small sticks as there are children. He shakes his head as he listens to the quarreling. At his feet is a pile of small sticks, at least one for each child.

FIRST CHILD: Why should I clean the barn? You're bigger than I am.

SECOND CHILD: Why should I milk cows and carry heavy pails? You're older than I am.

THIRD CHILD: Why should I scrub your dirty clothes and lift tubs of hot water?

FOURTH CHILD: I'd rather scrub clothes than plow when it's hot.

(Actors complain about other chores. The words "I" and "You" and general idea of discord give the idea of a fighting family. After a minute or so Farmer holds up his hands.)

FARMER *(yelling)*: Quiet!

FARMER: Sit down!

(Children sit on benches. Farmer stands between them.)

FARMER: I'm tired of your fighting. I want you to think. Why do we farm?

FIRST CHILD: We have to eat.

SECOND CHILD: We need wool for clothes.

THIRD CHILD: We need wood for the fire.

FOURTH CHILD: We need money.

FARMER: Oh, we need money. Why do we need money?

FIFTH CHILD: Taxes.

(*Children give two or three more answers. Last Child on bench, one nearest the audience, yells.*)

LAST CHILD: We need money to buy *me* a farm. I want to get away from the rest of you.

(*Others yell,* "Buy me a farm.")

FIRST CHILD: When I get a farm, my wheat will be better than your wheat.

SECOND CHILD: My chickens will lay more than your chickens.

(*Each yells how his farm will be better than the others.*)

FARMER (*raising hands*): Quiet!

(*All are quiet. Farmer picks up the bundle of sticks. He looks at it intently. Walks in front of children so that each can see the bundle.*)

FARMER: What's this?

LAST CHILD: A bundle of sticks.

FARMER: Yes, a bundle of sticks tied together firmly. (*hands bundle to First Child*) Can you break this bundle of sticks?

(*First Child tries unsuccessfully to break bundle of sticks.*)

FARMER: Pass the bundle to your sister. See if she can break it.

(*The bundle of sticks is passed from Child to*

Child. Each Child tries to break the bundle and fails. Farmer takes bundle and holds it up.)

FARMER: There are seven sticks in this bundle. (*Of course, he says the correct number of children present.*) There are seven children in our family. Can you break the sticks when they are tied together firmly?

CHILDREN: No.

FARMER: Now I'll give you each one stick. (*does so*) Now—(*children look at Farmer closely*) can you break your stick? Try. (*Each child breaks a stick.*) What happens to your stick when it stands alone?

FIRST CHILD: We can break it.

FARMER: Exactly. Some day each of you will have a farm or business of your own. What will happen if you always fight each other?

LAST CHILD: We'll all go broke.

FARMER: Yes, if each stands alone, fighting his brothers and sisters, you'll all be broken one way or another. (*Children look at each other and nod.*)

(*Farmer picks up bundle of sticks.*)

FARMER: What will happen if you are bound together as a family?

LAST CHILD (*standing*): No one can break us!

OTHER CHILDREN: You're right! (*add other appropriate remarks*)

FARMER: What do we do now?

(*Actors decide on response.*)

STORYTELLER: What's the big idea?

United we're strong. Alone we're weak.

Who's Stronger?

Characters

NORTH WIND   PERSON
SUN

SCENE. *Outdoors. Sun is playing happily with a yo-yo, spinning a hula hoop, skipping rope slowly, or in some other gentle way. Person, wearing an unbuttoned coat, is sitting on a bench downstage left. Into this happy scene, rushes North Wind, howling wildly.*

NORTH WIND: Shuuuuuuuuuu! Shuuuuuuuuuu! Shuuuuuuuuuu!

SUN (*standing still and watching him a minute*): Well, who are you?

NORTH WIND (*pausing*): I'm the North Wind, strongest force on earth.

SUN: Is that so? I think you're a big blowhard.

NORTH WIND: Is that so? Who are you?

SUN: I'm the Sun.

NORTH WIND: Hmmm. Think you're bright, don't you?

SUN: Bright enough, and as strong as you are.

NORTH WIND: Strong as I am? Want to prove it?

SUN: Why not?

NORTH WIND: Want to fight?

SUN: No, fighting doesn't prove a thing.

NORTH WIND: Doesn't prove a thing? I'll show you how strong I am! (*doubles up fists*)

SUN: Wait a minute. Wait a minute. I have an idea.

NORTH WIND: What?

SUN: See that person sitting over there?

NORTH WIND: Yes.

SUN: See that coat?

NORTH WIND: Yes.

SUN: Well, the one who can get that person's coat off will be the winner.

NORTH WIND: That's easy! I'll blow off the coat. Then I'll blow off the buttons. You go first.

SUN: No, you go first.

NORTH WIND: No, you.

SUN: We'll flip a coin. Head's the winner. (*flips coin*) You go first.

(*Sun stands right stage, Wind races around, howling wildly. The more he races, the tighter Person holds the coat, turns up the collar, puts hands in sleeves, hugs arms close to body.*)

NORTH WIND: Well, I give up. You try.

SUN: All right. Here goes.

(*Wind stands right stage. Sun circles the Person, smiling sweetly. Person takes hands out of sleeves, turns down collar of coat, unbuttons coat, opens it, and at last takes it off, lays it on the bench. Person stretches in the sunshine.*)

NORTH WIND: You did it! You did it! You made the person take off the coat. Congratulations! (*extends hand*)

SUN (*shaking hands*): Thank you.

STORYTELLER: What's the big idea?

Gentle persuasion is stronger than force.

Rain or Shine

Characters

STORYTELLER   PENELOPE, wife of a potter
MRS. KAGDIS   HELEN, wife of a gardener
MR. PAPPAS

STORYTELLER: Our stage is divided into three scenes. Over here we have the home of Penelope and her husband, the potter. (*points to left stage front*)

(*Penelope enters with a large earthen jar. Looks at sun. Sets jar down and looks at sky again. She continues to do this slowly with other jars as Storyteller continues.*)

STORYTELLER: Over here is the home of Helen and her husband, the gardener. (*points right stage front*)

(*Helen who is watering plants and pulling weeds continues to work there as Storyteller continues.*)

STORYTELLER: The center of the stage is the home of Mr. Pappas, father of Penelope and Helen. Mrs. Kagdis greets him as he is leaving home, walking stick in hand.

(*Storyteller moves right stage front and stands quietly.*)

MRS. KAGDIS: Good morning, Mr. Pappas.

MR. PAPPAS: Good morning, Mrs. Kagdis.

MRS. KAGDIS: Where are you going, walking stick in hand?

MR. PAPPAS: I am going to visit my daughters.

MRS. KAGDIS: And how is Penelope, the wife of the potter?

MR. PAPPAS: I am going to find out. I am going to ask, "Is there anything I can do to help you?"

MRS. KAGDIS: And how is Helen, the wife of the gardener?

MR. PAPPAS: I am going to find out. I am going

to ask, "Is there anything I can do to help you?"

MRS. KAGDIS: Good luck, Mr. Pappas. I hope you find out how you can help each daughter.

MR. PAPPAS: Thank you, Mrs. Kagdis. Good-bye.

(*Mrs. Kagdis exits. Mr. Pappas stands up straight and walks swinging his cane. Storyteller steps toward center of stage.*)

STORYTELLER: Mr. Pappas walks and walks and at last he comes to the home of his daughter Penelope, wife of the potter.

(*Storyteller steps to the side of the stage. Mr. Pappas, who has been walking while Storyteller was speaking, does not travel in a straight line. He approaches Penelope by crossing the front of the stage.*

Penelope sees her father and runs toward him. He rushes to meet her. They hug each other, with cries of "Father!" "Penelope!" They talk fast with gestures for a few seconds. Then Mr. Pappas speaks clearly.)

MR. PAPPAS: Penelope, how is everything?

PENELOPE: Wonderful!

MR. PAPPAS: Are you happy with your husband, the potter?

PENELOPE: Oh, yes!

MR. PAPPAS: Is there anything I can do for you?

PENELOPE: Yes, Father, just one thing. Pray for sunshine. We need sunshine to dry our pottery. Pray for sunshine.

MR. PAPPAS: I'll do that daughter. Now I must say good-bye.

(They say "Good-bye," and Mr. Pappas starts toward the home of Helen. Storyteller steps toward center of stage.)

STORYTELLER: Mr. Pappas walks and walks and at last he reaches the home of his daughter Helen, wife of the gardener.

(Storyteller walks to other side of stage. Mr. Pappas does not walk in a straight line. He approaches the home of Helen by crossing the front of the stage.

Helen sees her father and runs to meet him. He rushes to meet her. They hug each other with cries of "Father!" "Helen!" They talk fast and gesture. Then Mr. Pappas speaks clearly.)

MR. PAPPAS: Helen! How is everything?

HELEN: Wonderful!

MR. PAPPAS: Are you happy with your husband, the gardener?

HELEN: Oh, yes!

MR. PAPPAS: Is there anything I can do for you?

HELEN: Oh, yes, Father. Just one thing. Pray for rain. Our gardens need rain. Please pray for rain!

(They say "Good-bye," and Mr. Pappas starts toward home, center front. Storyteller steps toward center of stage.)

STORYTELLER: Mr. Pappas leaves the home of his daughter, Helen, happily. But as he walks and walks, he becomes worried. His steps become slower. He begins to lean on his cane. (*Mr. Pappas pantomimes changes in his gait as Storyteller speaks.*) At last he reaches his home. Mrs. Kagdis is there to greet him.

(*Storyteller steps to side of stage.*)

MRS. KAGDIS: Mr. Pappas! What is wrong?

MR. PAPPAS: I have a problem, a real problem.

MRS. KAGDIS: What is it? Didn't you see your daughter, Penelope, wife of the potter?

MR. PAPPAS: Oh, yes, I saw my daughter Penelope, wife of the potter. She asked me to pray for sunny weather.

MRS. KAGDIS: So?

MR. PAPPAS: I promised to pray for sunny weather. Then I went to the home of my daughter Helen, wife of the gardener.

MRS. KAGDIS: Yes?

MR. PAPPAS: My daughter Helen, wife of the gardener asked me to pray for rain. Her garden needs rain.

MRS. KAGDIS: So?

MR. PAPPAS: I started home. Then I remembered: I had promised Penelope I'd pray for sunshine, and I'd promised Helen I'd pray for rain. How can I make both daughters happy when one wants sunshine and one wants rain? What am I going to do?

LET'S FIND THE BIG IDEA

MRS. KAGDIS (*shaking her head and speaking softly*): I don't know. You do have a problem.

STORYTELLER: What's the big idea?

You can't please everyone at the same time.

Playlets

A playlet is often a scene in which something happens, the acting out of a single incident. The plot, if there is one, is very simple.

Characters in a playlet, unlike those in a skit, are more than types. Each one has a personality. The audience must be able to sense this individuality, not only by the way each actor walks and talks, but also by the way he or she reacts to other characters and to the situation in the playlet.

Like the skits in this book, each playlet has a big idea that the actors must get across to the audience. Look at the introduction of skits for some tips on how to do this (page 13). Make sure that listeners can hear and understand the lines that will help them get the big idea of the playlet.

So Proud

Characters

JACQUES, a miller's
  horse
PRINCE, a merchant's
  horse

FIRST ROBBER
SECOND ROBBER

SCENE. *A green pasture outside a French inn long ago. Prince is eating. He wears a beautiful harness. His saddlebags are richly decorated. Jacques enters. He has a plain saddle and brown cloth saddlebags.*

JACQUES: Good morning.

PRINCE (*staring at new horse*): Well, who are you?

JACQUES: I'm Jacques, the miller's horse.

PRINCE: I can see that you are a farmer's horse or a miller's horse—old leather harness, lumpy cloth saddlebags.

JACQUES: I carry flour. That's what's important.

PRINCE: Flour! Only a horse like you would carry flour!

JACQUES: Well, what do you carry?

PRINCE: Can't you guess? (*doesn't wait for an answer*) My owner is a merchant. So I carry silks and jewels, silver and gold dishes, and other expensive things. I'm proud of what I carry.

38

JACQUES: I can see that!

PRINCE: In fact, I am so proud that I don't want to eat with you.

JACQUES: Our masters eat at the same inn.

PRINCE: But not at the same table. I'll eat here where the grass is greenest. You eat over there.

JACQUES: All right. But first let me tell you something. I'm proud, too, in a different way. I'm proud to carry flour because my master needs flour. I don't need to be a big show-off to be proud.

(Jacques goes right stage. Robbers enter. Look around. First Robber points to Prince. Robbers are delighted. Second Robber points to Jacques. Pantomimes, "Shall we get him?" First Robber shakes his head. Pantomimes, "We'll work together to take the rich horse." They sneak up to Prince and lead him offstage. Prince neighs loudly.

In a few seconds, Prince returns without his saddlebags.)

JACQUES: What are you carrying now, proud horse?

PRINCE: Nothing.

JACQUES: Are you proud?

(Actors decide how Prince reacts.)

STORYTELLER: What's the big idea?

A show-off invites trouble.

Lion, Sick and Dying?

Characters

KING LION   GOAT
CUB LION   SHEEP
FOX   CALF

SCENE. *King Lion and Cub Lion are in front of King Lion's den.*

CUB LION: Daddy, I'm hungry.

KING LION: So am I, but I don't feel like hunting.

CUB LION: What'll we do?

KING LION: I know, make the animals come to us. We can eat them right here.

CUB LION: How can you do that?

KING LION: Let me think. (*pauses*) I know. Go tell the animals that I, King Lion, am sick and dying. I want them to come one by one and listen to my last will and testament.

CUB LION: Good idea, Daddy, Good luck!

(*Cub Lion runs offstage. King Lion yawns, and stretches. Cub Lion returns.*)

CUB LION: I told them, Daddy I told them.

KING LION: Good! Good! When they come, tell them again that I am sick and dying. Send them into my cave, one by one.

CUB LION: All right, Daddy. Here comes Fox.

40

(*King Lion darts into his cave. Fox enters.*)

FOX: Good day, Cub Lion.

CUB LION: Good day, friend Fox.

FOX: I hear that you daddy, King Lion, is sick and dying.

CUB LION: Oh, yes, please go into his cave and hear his last will and testament. He wants to remember you.

FOX: Thank you, Cub Lion. It's kind of your father to think of me. But I think I better rest a little before I visit him. I'm all out of wind. I'll relax over here.

CUB LION: All right, friend Fox. Here comes friend Goat.

(*Fox goes to the side of the stage. Goat enters.*)

GOAT: Good day, Cub Lion.

CUB LION: Good day, friend Goat.

GOAT: I hear that your daddy, King Lion, is sick and dying.

CUB LION: Oh, yes, please go into his cave and hear his last will and testament. He wants to remember you.

(*Goat goes into cave.*)

GOAT: (*inside cave*): Maaaaaaaa!

(*Enter Sheep.*)

SHEEP: Good day, Cub Lion.

CUB LION: Good day, friend Sheep.

SHEEP: I hear that your daddy, King Lion, is sick and dying.

CUB LION: Oh, yes, please go into his cave and

hear his last will and testament. He wants to remember you.

(*Sheep goes into cave.*)

SHEEP (*inside cave*): Baaaaaa!

(*Enter Calf.*)

CALF: Good day, Cub Lion.

CUB LION: Good day, friend Calf.

CALF: I hear that your daddy, King Lion, is sick and dying.

CUB LION: Oh, yes, please go into his cave and hear his last will and testament. He wants very much to remember you.

(*Calf goes into cave.*)

CALF (*from inside cave*): Mooooooo!

(*Fox comes center stage just as King Lion is coming out of his cave. Fox starts to turn away.*)

KING LION: Fox!

(*Fox turns.*)

FOX: Oh, yes, your Majesty. Good day, your Majesty.

KING LION: Didn't you hear that I am sick and dying?

FOX: Oh, yes. I'm sorry, sir.

KING LION: Why didn't you come into my cave? Goat, Sheep, and Calf all came into my cave to hear my last will and testament.

FOX: I know, sir.

KING LION: Then why didn't you come into my cave?

FOX: Because, sir, I saw Goat, Sheep, and Calf go into your cave, but I didn't see anyone come out. I didn't want to crowd you in your cave, especially when you are sick and dying. I think I'll wait right here until I see the other animals come out of your cave.

KING LION (*crouching*): Grrrrrr—

FOX: On second thought, I think I'll leave now. Good-bye.

(*Exits in a hurry.*)

STORYTELLER: What's the big idea?

Don't believe everything you hear.

The Country Mouse and the City Mouse

Characters

ANDERS, a city mouse CAT
OLE, a country mouse OLGA, a maid
LADY OF THE HOUSE

SCENE 1. *A woods in Sweden in autumn. Ole is picking seeds. Enter Anders.*

OLE: Hello, who are you?

ANDERS: I'm Anders. Who are you?

OLE: Ole. You look like a stranger.

ANDERS: That's right. I am a stranger.

OLE: Where do you live?

ANDERS: In a very nice house in the city. I have everything I want.

OLE: Why are you here?

ANDERS: I got to thinking, How does a field mouse live? So I took a long walk, and here I am.

OLE: Welcome! Would you like to see my home? *(points to small nest under a tree root)*

ANDERS: You mean you live in that hole in the ground? *(Ole nods.)* Well, no thank you! Let's talk right here.

OLE: All right. What shall we talk about?

ANDERS: Food. I'm hungry.

OLE: In that case, let's eat. I gathered these seeds for winter. Share them with me now.

(He passes bag of seeds to Anders who takes some, nibbles on them, and makes a face.)

ANDERS: You call this food? *(Ole nods.)* Is this all that you have to eat?

OLE: Well, no—but, yes, this time of year, more or less—

ANDERS: What do you mean?

OLE: This time of year I live on seeds and tiny nuts, anything I can find. In fact, I store some for winter.

ANDERS: Don't you go outdoors in winter?

OLE: Not much when there's snow. I don't like to run around in the snow.

ANDERS: I know, too cold.

OLE: Well, more than that. It's easy for an owl or hawk to spot me against the white snow.

ANDERS (*shocked*): An owl or a hawk? You have to look out for an owl or a hawk? (*Ole nods.*) Oh, really, you should come and see how I live. I have a nice warm house, right next to the kitchen. All the cheese, bread, and cake I can eat. I'm never afraid of an owl or a hawk. Really, you should come and live with me. I have a very happy home.

OLE: I'd like to visit you. I'd like to see your happy home.

ANDERS: Great! Come for Christmas.

OLE: Thank you.

(*Ole and Anders say "Good-bye" to each other.*)

SCENE 2. *Home of Anders in the city at Christmas time. On a table, center front, there's cake, cheese, and bread. Anders is tasting this and that. He hears* "scratch, scratch." *Runs to door.*

ANDERS: Ole! Come in! Welcome to my happy home!

OLE: Thank you. It's good to be here. That was a long walk from the country. I'm hungry!

ANDERS: Help yourself to some goodies.

OLE (*seeing food*): Ohhhhhh!

ANDERS: What did I tell you? All the cake, cheese, and bread you can eat. Help yourself.

(*They start to nibble.*)

OLE: Oh, this is good! I never ate anything like this! You do have a happy home!

(*They continue to nibble and soon hear singing offstage.*)

LADY OF THE HOUSE (*offstage*): Tra-la-la-la-la!

ANDERS: Quick! The lady of the house! Hide!

(*Mice scurry to edge of room. Enter Lady of the House.*)

LADY OF THE HOUSE: Beautiful! Beautiful! Everything set for the Christmas party. (*looks at table carefully*) Crumbs? Where did they come from? I must call the maid. Olga! Olga! (*exits*)

(*Ole and Anders come front stage, fanning themselves.*)

ANDERS: Wow! That was a close call.

(*Cat enters and creeps slowly toward mice.*)

OLE: Worse than an owl or a hawk.

ANDERS: At least she made more noise than a bird. That's the good thing about people. They make noise and let you know they're coming.

OLE: You're right. It's easy to keep away from hunters.

ANDERS: What I really worry about is the— (*looks around and sees Cat; screams*) Cat! Run, Ole, run!

(*Mice run around room with Cat chasing them.*)

Olga enters. At first she sees only Cat because mice race to edge of room.)

OLGA (*chasing Cat*): Get out of here! Get out of here! Don't touch that food.

(*Cat runs out of room. Olga relaxes a minute. Then she sees mice.*)

OLGA: Eeeeek! Mice! (*exits*)

(*Anders and Ole come front stage.*)

OLE: Wow!

ANDERS: Yes, wow! Luckily she didn't have a broom.

OLE: Luckily you saw the cat in time.

ANDERS: Luckily the Lady of the House didn't set a trap next to the cheese.

OLE: You call this a happy home? You can't even eat in peace.

ANDERS: Well, I know, but— I do have—

OLE: What?

(*Anders looks sad.*)

OLE: I'm sorry. I'm a poor guest. Enjoy what you have, Anders, my city cousin. But I am going back to my country home, eat my seeds, and look out for owls and hawks. I like my country home.

ANDERS: Thank you for coming, Ole, my country cousin. I like my city home.

STORYTELLER: What's the big idea?

What's good for you may be misery for someone else.

The Heart of a Monkey

Characters

MONKEY   SHARK

SCENE. *At the edge of the island of Zanzibar. Monkey is in a tree left front. Shark is in the water.*

SHARK: Good morning, Monkey.

MONKEY: Good morning, Shark. Would you like a kooyoo nut?

SHARK: No, thank you. I don't like kooyoo nuts.

MONKEY: You don't like kooyoo nuts? Other sharks like kooyoo nuts. You must be a stranger.

SHARK: Yes, I am a stranger, but I've heard about you. I hear that you are very nice.

MONKEY: Thank you.

SHARK: I hear that every day you throw kooyoo nuts to sharks.

MONKEY: That's right. I do.

SHARK: The sharks want to repay you for your kindness.

MONKEY: Repay me? How?

SHARK: Be our guest. Visit us at our home.

MONKEY: Me? Monkey? Visit the home of a shark? No, I'm very happy right here.

SHARK (*slowly*): Are you really happy? Have you thought about being happy? Do you know what you are missing?

49

MONKEY: Well, not really.

SHARK: How can you know that you are happy if you stay here? Wouldn't you like to see more of the world?

MONKEY: Maybe I'd like to see more of the world, but how can I leave an island?

SHARK: That's easy. I'll carry you. Get on my back.

MONKEY: Me? Monkey, ride on the back of a shark?

SHARK: Sure! Why not!

MONKEY: That sounds like fun! Let's go!

(*Monkey gets on back of shark. They ride a little way, humming a tune. Shark stops.*)

SHARK: Monkey, I must tell you something.

MONKEY: Why bother? This is fun!

SHARK (*sharply*): Monkey, before we go any farther, I must tell you the truth. Our chief is very sick. The only medicine that will help him is the heart of a monkey.

MONKEY (*pretending to be sad*): That's too bad. I'm sorry your chief is very sick. (*pauses to think*) You were foolish not to tell me before we started.

SHARK: Why? (*Monkey hesitates.*) Tell me. (*no reply*) Why don't you speak?

MONKEY: There's nothing to say now. It's too late.

SHARK: Too late?

MONKEY: Yes, I don't have my heart with me. If

you had told me the truth before we started, I would have brought my heart with me.

SHARK (*yelling*): What!

MONKEY: Shhhhhh! It's a monkey secret. When a monkey leaves home, he hangs his heart on a tree. Right now my heart is hanging on a tree.

SHARK: Your heart is hanging on a tree?

MONKEY: Yes. I see you don't believe me. You think I'm scared. So let's go on to your home. You can kill me and look for my heart, but you won't find it unless—

SHARK: Unless what?

MONKEY: Unless you turn around and take me back to my tree. (*pauses*) I am sorry about your chief. I know that he needs the heart of a monkey, and my heart is on my tree.

SHARK: You are right! My chief needs the heart of a monkey. Let's go back and get your heart.

(*Shark turns around with Monkey on his back. They travel fast. When they come to the tree, Monkey jumps into tree. He is quiet.*)

SHARK: Monkey! Monkey! Get your heart. Come quickly.

(*no answer*)

SHARK: Come, Monkey, let's be going.

MONKEY: Where?

SHARK: To my home, of course.

MONKEY: To your home? Forget it! Even a monkey doesn't make the same mistake twice.

STORYTELLER: What's the big idea?

Never accept a ride from a stranger.

When in a jam, think fast.

Problems! Problems!

Characters

RAGGED PEDDLER   BALD VILLAGER
FIRST VILLAGER   OLD VILLAGER
HUNCHBACK   FIFTH VILLAGER
RED HEAD
AS MANY OTHER VILLAGERS AS PRACTICAL

SCENE. *A village in a valley in the Near East many years ago. Some villagers are standing in groups of two or three, talking softly and gesturing that everything is bad. A few are doing simple tasks, such as whittling or mending. Others may be trudging slowly, basket over an arm or on head. Old Villager sits right front, leaning on a cane, swaying a little, grumbling.*

Offstage, on either side, is a sturdy hook fastened to a stationary object. At the correct time, actors stretch a clothesline across the stage and fasten ends to the hooks.

Ragged Peddler enters left, whistling or humming happily. He steps briskly and stands left of center stage to look around.

Villagers glare at him and shake their heads. He is a strange-looking person with ragged clothes, mostly bright patches, a clothesline slung over one shoulder, and a pack on his back. In the pack is a triangle and a clapper and a bag of clothespins.

First Villager enters left, slumped over, grumpy looking. Peddler speaks to him and then to some others one by one.

PEDDLER: Good morning!

FIRST VILLAGER: What's good about it? (*continues to walk across stage*)

(*Peddler goes to Hunchback who looks up from his whittling.*)

PEDDLER: Hello. How are you?

HUNCHBACK: I'll tell you. I'm rotten. The hump on my back makes me sick.

(*Peddler goes to Red Head who looks up from her mending.*)

PEDDLER: Excuse me, fair miss.

RED HEAD: Fair miss? Well, I guess I look better than you do!

(*Peddler approaches Old Villager and stands a little right of center stage.*)

PEDDLER: Please tell me, wise one.

OLD VILLAGER: Wise one? Why wise one?

PEDDLER: Because I can see that you have lived a long time.

OLD VILLAGER: It's my cane. (*stands and waves cane*) You don't like my cane. I'll tell you something. I don't like this cane either. What do you want to know about my cane?

PEDDLER (*calmly*): I don't want to know anything about your cane. I want to know something about this village. Everyone seems to be unhappy.

OLD VILLAGER: Everyone is unhappy.

(*A few villagers gather on either side of Peddler, who is near center stage. Gradually they become interested.*)

PEDDLER: Why are they unhappy? This is a beautiful valley. The sun shines like gold on the mountain.

(*Villagers nod, disgusted.*)

FIRST VILLAGER: What good does that do?

PEDDLER: The land looks fertile.

BALD VILLAGER: Good enough, I guess. No one starves.

PEDDLER: Everyone is well clothed. (*Villagers nod.*) Has there been an epidemic of any disease? (*Villagers shake heads.*) Are you free to come and go? (*Villagers nod.*)

(*Peddler turns to Old Villager and speaks slowly and loudly.*)

PEDDLER: Then why is everyone unhappy? What is the problem?

OLD VILLAGER: I'ts not one problem. Everyone has his own problem. Each person thinks his problem is the worst.

PEDDLER: So—It's problems that make them unhappy. How lucky that I came! I know how to make everyone happy.

(*Peddler takes a triangle and clapper out of his*

pack and strikes it a few times. He calls out in a sing-song voice.)

PEDDLER: Come! Come, all in distress.

I can give you happiness!

(Actors form a semicircle with Peddler in center so that he can speak to each one.)

PEDDLER: Now, one by one you can tell me your problems.

OLD VILLAGER: I told you. I hate walking with a cane!

RED HEAD: I hate my red hair!

HUNCHBACK: I hate my hunchback!

BALD VILLAGER: I hate my bald head!

FIRST VILLAGER: I hate my neighbor. Such a fuss-budget!

FIFTH VILLAGER: I hate my neighbor's dog. Barks all the time.

(As many villagers as feasible tell about individual problems. This scene must move fast. Each actor continues to pantomime about his problem after he has spoken.)

(Peddler strikes triangle again.)

PEDDLER: All right. We agree. Everyone in this village has a special problem. Now, this is what I want you to do. Take my long rope. *(He unwinds his long rope quickly and hands the ends to two people.)* Stretch this line across the village green like a clothesline.

(Two Villagers do this quickly by fastening ends

to offstage hooks. Peddler takes a bag of clothes-pins from his pack. Villagers murmur and gesture, "What's he doing?" "He's crazy!" and other appropriate remarks. When all Villagers are again on stage, Peddler speaks.)

PEDDLER: Now, I want everyone to hang his problem on this line and come right back here.

(Villagers do so quickly. The Villager with a fuss-budget neighbor runs offstage and returns quickly with a stuffed dummy or a life-sized picture of a person. Another villager does the same with a dog. Red Head takes off a wig and hangs it on the line. Hunchback takes pillow from under his coat, and so on. Villagers who did not explain their problem also hang symbols on the line. Soon the line is filled. Peddler strikes triangle. Everyone pays attention.)

PEDDLER: I see. Everyone has hung his problem on the line. *(Villagers nod.)* That's great, except it isn't real. We all know that in this life no one is free from problems. *(Villagers agree.)* Everyone has a personal problem.

However, I now give you one chance—a chance of a lifetime. Just this once, you may choose your problem. You *(speaking to Red Head)*—you didn't like your red hair. *(She nods.)* But you must have a problem. Go take a problem off the line. It's yours.

(Red Head goes to line, looks up and down. Takes her red wig and puts it on.)

57

(*Peddler turns to person who didn't like his neighbor.*)

PEDDLER: You didn't like your fuss-budget neighbor. She's out of your life. Go choose another problem.

(*Villager looks at problems. Takes down his fuss-budget neighbor. Quickly each person takes back his own problem. Peddler strikes triangle again.*)

PEDDLER: I see. Everyone has his own original problem. Why did you choose your red hair?

RED HEAD: Things could be worse.

(*Villagers agree among themselves.*)

PEDDLER: You really think things could be worse?

VILLAGERS (*happily*): Yes, Yes! Things could be worse!

PEDDLER: Then I'll be on my way. But I'll leave my clothesline here as a reminder. Everyone has a problem. Some problems are worse than your own. Good-bye! (*exits*)

STORYTELLER: What's the big idea?

Cheer up! Things could be worse.

The Law of the Jungle

Characters

JAN, judge who walks
   on two feet
MESSENGERS
WEAVER BIRD
PARROT
OSTRICH
GIRAFFE
ZEBRA

ELEPHANT
ANT
MUZIMU, wizard of
   jungle
GUARDS, who are also
   drummers
OTHER ANIMALS
   AND BIRDS,
   as many as practical

SCENE. *Jungle, Africa. Jan sits on a stump center, a few feet from the front of the stage, eating nuts, or pretending to do so. A Guard, holding a drum, sits on either side of Jan.*

Animals and Birds are milling around at back of stage, each walking or flapping wings in his own way. (You can identify characters by having them wear signs or simple, symbolic costumes. They must not wear masks that cover the face. Voices must be heard.)

Messengers enter and bow to Jan.

JAN: Welcome, Messengers. Why have you come?

FIRST MESSENGER: Oh, wise judge, someone has torn the nest of Weaver Bird.

SECOND MESSENGER: She has many friends. They demand justice.

JAN: Weaver Bird shall have justice. The culprit will be punished. Guards, beat the drums. Let the birds and beasts know that I am holding court.

(*Guards beat drums. Animals and Birds form a semicircle with Jan in the center. As each character steps forward to speak, he faces Jan sideways, not with his back to the audience. In this position, he throws his voice to a back corner of the audience.*)

FIRST MESSENGER (*raising arms*): Silence!

(*Guards stop beating drums, go to back of stage.*)

FIRST MESSENGER: Birds and beasts, let the good and wise judge, Jan, hear the story of Weaver Bird.

(*Weaver Bird steps forward.*)

JAN: Speak, Weaver Bird.

WEAVER BIRD: Oh, wise Jan, judge of the jungle, I am Weaver Bird. I build a fancy and pretty nest with many kinds of grasses woven together in a very special way. Members of my family live together in one tree, each with a separate nest. For years we have lived in peace and worked hard. Now our work is useless.

JAN: Why is that?

WEAVER BIRD: Someone comes time after time and tears our nests apart. Sometimes he kills young birds. I think Parrot is guilty. Shame on you, Parrot.

61

OTHER BIRDS AND ANIMALS: Shame on you, Parrot!

JAN: Quiet! Do not prejudge anyone. Parrot, step forward and confess.

(*Parrot steps forward.*)

PARROT: Your honor, I didn't do it. I think Ostrich did it.

JAN: Ostrich, step forward.

(*Ostrich steps forward. Parrot stands to right of Jan. After each animal or bird has finished speaking, he stands to the right of Jan. Other animals move to the right, making way for him. With characters standing in order of speaking, Jan can pronounce his sentence easily, naming each bird or animal in turn.*)

OSTRICH: Your honor, I didn't do it. I can't reach that nest. I think Giraffe did it.

JAN: Giraffe, step forward.

(*Giraffe steps forward as Ostrich takes his place next to Parrot.*)

GIRAFFE: Your honor, I didn't do it. I think Zebra knows something about it.

JAN: Zebra, step forward!

(*Zebra steps forward as Giraffe takes his place next to Ostrich.*)

ZEBRA: I didn't do it. I can't climb a tree or reach the nest. Maybe Elephant did it.

JAN: Elephant step forward!

(*Zebra takes his place next to Giraffe as Elephant steps forward.*)

ELEPHANT: Your honor, why should I bother a little bird? Call Ant. He crawls everywhere.

JAN: Ant, step forward!

(*Ant steps forward as Elephant takes his place next to Zebra.*)

ANT: Your honor, how could I tear apart a bird's nest?

JAN (*standing*): Enough of this nonsense. How can I find the culprit? Maybe you are all guilty. Hear my sentence. When I give the command I want: Parrot to peck Ostrich, Ostrich to bite Giraffe, Giraffe to kick Zebra, Zebra to butt Elephant, Elephant to blow on Ant, Ant to sting Parrot. Form a big circle.

(*Jan steps to right stage front. Animals and Birds who were accused form a big circle.*)

JAN: Now, obey me!

(*Birds and animals who were sentenced go around in a circle, pretending to bite, kick, or butt each other. They let out wild cries. Other Birds and Animals yell, "More!" or make noises of the jungle.*

Suddenly, Guards beat drums wildly. Animals and Birds are quiet. They separate, forming an aisle down the center of the stage.

Enter Muzimu. He raises his arms. Other characters bow.)

MUZIMU: Look up! (*Other characters do so.*) What is happening?

JAN: Oh, great wizard, Weaver Bird had a problem, so she came to me, Jan, the wise judge, seeking justice.

MUZIMU: What was your problem, Weaver Bird?

WEAVER BIRD: Someone tore my nest apart, time after time. I think Parrot did it.

PARROT: I think Ostrich did it.

OSTRICH: I think Giraffe did it.

GIRAFFE: I think Zebra did it.

ZEBRA: I think Elephant did it.

ELEPHANT: I think Ant did it.

MUZIMU (*to Jan*): How did you find the culprit?

JAN: I didn't find the culprit, but I administered justice.

MUZIMU: How?

JAN: I ordered Parrot to peck Ostrich, Ostrich to bite Giraffe, Giraffe to kick Zebra, Zebra to butt Elephant, Elephant to blow on Ant, Ant to sting Parrot.

MUZIMU: You ordered the beasts and birds to bite and kick and butt each other?

JAN: Yes.

MUZIMU: You call that justice?

JAN: Yes. It must be justice. What I say must be justice. I am Jan, wise judge of the jungle.

MUZIMU: Wise judge? What makes you think you are a *wise* judge?

JAN: Because I stand on two feet. No other animal stands on two feet. I'm different, so I must be wise.

MUZIMU: You are a fool! A fool with wisdom in your feet. From this day on, you shall swing from trees and walk bent over. You shall be a monkey, and your cousins will be chimpanzees and baboons. No one will again mistake you for a wise judge.

WEAVER BIRD: What about the rest of us? What will we do without Jan, the judge?

MUZIMU: You can do one of three things:
Learn to live together in peace;
choose a judge who is really wise; or
live as best you can by the law of the jungle,
biting, kicking, and hurting each other.
Good-bye.

(*Guards beat drums. Muzimu exists. Jan walks across the stage acting like a monkey. Other characters exit, each walking in his own way. Actors decide whether characters go away peacefully or exit fighting each other.*)

STORYTELLER: What's the big idea?

Don't choose a leader by his looks.

Being different is not the same as being wise.

65

Plays

A play is a dramatization of a struggle. There is a problem; as the plot unfolds, the audience understands why the situation is important to the characters involved.

Producing a good play demands teamwork. There will be lead roles, supporting cast, and bit parts. All actors must work together to bring about a climax or high point of the play.

Each actor must study the character to be portrayed and understand how the individual helps to bring out the big idea that underlies the production. Each actor must try to think and therefore act like the personality involved in the story. But even as the actor plays the part of an individual, he must think of the success of the entire play.

Every member of the cast must pay attention to what is being said and done, never calling attention to himself or falling out of character. If a lead speaker gives an incorrect cue or seems to forget a line, the supportive cast ad-lib (make up speech) or pantomime until the play is back on track.

All the cast should display enthusiasm, despair, joy, disgust, or whatever emotion the script calls for, working together to put a big idea across to the audience.

Crowded?

Characters

NAOMI   DUCK
JOSEF, her husband   DONKEY
BABY, their child   GOAT
RABBI

SCENE. *Home of a Jewish farm family in eastern Europe a hundred years ago. A cradle stands center front. Baby is heard, but not seen. A table with a basket of dry washing is near the cradle. Other furniture makes the room look crowded.*

As the scene opens Baby is crying loudly. Naomi tries frantically to quiet the child.

BABY: Waaaa! Waaaa! Waaaa!

NAOMI: Quiet, Baby, quiet!

BABY: Waaaa! Waaaa! Waaaa!

NAOMI: Baby, be quiet. Can't you see? I can't rock you. There's no room for a rocking chair. This house is too crowded!

BABY: Waaaa! Waaaa! Waaaa!

(*Naomi rocks back and forth in despair. Josef enters.*)

BABY: Waaaa! Waaaa! Waaaa!

NAOMI: Baby is crying.

JOSEF: I know. Why don't you do something?

NAOMI: What can I do? I can't rock Baby.

There's no room for a chair. The house is too crowded.

BABY: Waaaa! Waaaa! Waaaa!

NAOMI: What can I do in a crowded house?

JOSEF: I don't *know*. I *don't* know. I'll get the Rabbi. He'll tell us what to do.

BABY: Waaaa! Waaaa! Waaaa!

NAOMI: Go at once. Get the Rabbi.

(*Baby continues to cry. Naomi makes frantic gestures. Rabbi and Josef enter.*)

NAOMI: Rabbi, wise Rabbi, this place is too crowded. I can't take care of the Baby. The Baby cries all the time. What can we do about a house that's too crowded?

(*Baby cries again. Rabbi looks around.*)

RABBI: Let me think. (*pauses*) Do you own a duck?

JOSEF: Yes, we own a duck.

RABBI: Then go and get Duck. Bring her inside this room. (*exits*)

NAOMI: What! Duck in this room?

JOSEF: Naomi, we must obey the Rabbi. I'll get Duck.

(*Baby cries again. Naomi rocks back and forth in despair. Josef enters with Duck. Duck waves wings wildly. Hops all over the place. Naomi and Josef chase it. At last Duck settles down in a corner.*)

NAOMI: Now, what good did that do?

69

JOSEF: I don't *know*. I *don't* know. I'll get the Rabbi. He'll tell us what to do.

(*Baby again cries. Naomi keeps saying, "Shhhhh!" Duck flaps in corner saying, "Quack!" Rabbi and Josef enter.*)

NAOMI: Oh, Rabbi, wise Rabbi, we got the Duck. She flapped about. The place is still crowded. What shall we do?

RABBI: Let me think. (*pauses*) Do you own a donkey?

JOSEF: Yes, we own a donkey.

RABBI: Then go get the Donkey. Bring him into the house. (*exits*)

NAOMI: What good will that do?

JOSEF: Naomi, we must obey the Rabbi. I'll get the Donkey.

(*Josef exits. Again there is a brief wild scene as Baby cries, Naomi is going crazy, Duck quacks. Josef enters with Donkey.*)

DONKEY: Hee-haw! Hee-haw! Hee-haw! (*He continues to bray as he kicks up his legs, bumps into furniture. Naomi and Josef chase Donkey until he at last sits in a corner near Duck with a long, loud "Heeee-haw!"*)

NAOMI: What good did that do? The place is still crowded.

JOSEF: I don't *know*. I *don't* know. I'll get the Rabbi. He'll tell us what to do.

(*Again Baby cries, Naomi is going crazy. Duck*

quacks, and Donkey brays, "Hee-haw!" *Josef enters with Rabbi.*)

NAOMI: Oh, Rabbi, wise Rabbi, we got the Donkey. He kicked everything. The place is still crowded. What shall we do?

RABBI: Let me think. (*pauses*) Do you own a goat?

JOSEF: Yes, we own a goat.

RABBI: Then go get the Goat. Bring him into the house. (*exits*)

NAOMI: What good will that do?

JOSEF: Naomi, we must obey the Rabbi. I'll get the Goat.

(*Again Baby cries, Naomi is going crazy. Duck quacks. Donkey brays. Josef enters with Goat. Goat goes directly to basket of clothes and begins to pull them out and chew them.*)

NAOMI: Stop! Stop! Stop! My washing! My good clean washing! Stop!

(*Josef helps her chase Goat into the corner with other animals.*)

NAOMI: What good did that do?

JOSEF: I don't *know*. I *don't* know. I'll get the Rabbi. He'll tell us what to do.

(*Josef exits. Again Baby cries. Naomi is going crazy. Duck, Donkey, and Goat cry out from the corner. Josef and Rabbi enter.*)

NAOMI: Oh, Rabbi, wise Rabbi, we got the Goat.

He chewed up my wash. The house is still crowded. What shall we do?

RABBI: Let me think. (*pauses*) Chase all the animals out of the house.

(*Rabbi exits. Josef and Naomi shoo animals out of the door.*)

NAOMI: What do you know? The place isn't crowded anymore.

JOSEF: The room looks empty.

NAOMI: Very empty. Let's ask my sister and her children to come here for a visit.

(*Josef nods. Naomi nods. Baby cries sweetly,* "Cooo! Cooo!")

STORYTELLER: What's the big idea?

Things aren't always as bad as you think they are.

Anyone Could, But—

Characters

LORD CHAMBERLAIN   TWO PEASANT
KING   WOMEN
TWO SHEPHERDS   TWO MERCHANTS
                            SANDY

SCENE. *A road. Stone in the middle of the road. (This can be a box, covered to resemble a stone.) Lord Chamberlain and King stand on either side of the stone.*

LORD CHAMBERLAIN: Your Highness, I do not understand. Why did you dig a hole in the road, put a purse with gold in the hole, and then put this huge stone above the gold? The stone is in the way.

KING: Yes, it is. But this stone may help me find a certain person.

LORD CHAMBERLAIN: Your Highness, are you feeling well? Is your head all right?

KING: Never fear, Lord Chamberlain. My head is well. My heart is heavy. You see, I am worried about my people.

LORD CHAMBERLAIN: I can understand that. They bring you every little problem that they have.

KING: That's true.

LORD CHAMBERLAIN: They depend on you for everything.

74

KING: That's just the trouble. They depend on me too much. I think they have forgotten how to help themselves. I think they have forgotten how to help one another.

LORD CHAMBERLAIN: But what good is a stone in the road?

KING: You'll see. Shh! Here come two shepherds returning from market. Let's hide. (*They exit.*)

FIRST SHEPHERD: Just look at that! A stone in the road!

SECOND SHEPHERD: Of all things! Thank goodness, it wasn't there this morning!

FIRST SHEPHERD: That's right. The sheep would have had to go around.

SECOND SHEPHERD: I hope someone tells the king about this before next market day.

FIRST SHEPHERD: I hope he gets it out of the way—and fast!

(*Shepherds exit complaining. King and Lord Chamberlain enter.*)

KING: See what I mean?

LORD CHAMBERLAIN: I think so. Shhh! Here come two peasant women.

(*Lord Chamberlain and King exit. Women appear.*)

FIRST WOMAN: Well, a nice kettle of fish!

SECOND WOMAN: Not fish, sister. Not fish, but a mighty ugly stone in the road.

FIRST WOMAN: Glad it isn't dark. I might have stubbed my toe.

SECOND WOMAN: Might do worse than that. What is this world coming to? A stone in the road! Where is the king?

(*Women exit. Merchants enter.*)

FIRST MERCHANT: Yes, business was good, very good. But look! What is this? A stone in the road.

SECOND MERCHANT: I wonder if the authorities have been notified.

FIRST MERCHANT: The king must be slipping, allowing a stone to remain in the middle of the road.

(*Merchants exit complaining. Sandy enters whistling or humming.*)

SANDY: Wow! Look at that stone! Right in the middle of the road. Lucky I saw it before it got dark. Someone might have bumped into it and got hurt. Wonder if I can move it. Let's see. If I push here, it will roll down there. Nothing's in the way. (*pushes stone*) There! (*stone disappears*) There she rolls. (*looks down; gasps*) Hey! What's in the hole? Gold! It must be the king's gold. No one else has that much gold! Wonder if someone stole it. I must tell the king. What shall I do? I can't carry it all. I must get help.

KING (*appearing*): Wait. I've been looking for you.

SANDY: Oh, your Highness, I just found this gold. I didn't steal it, sir. Honest, I didn't. There was a stone here. I rolled it away. Believe me, sir!

KING: I believe you, because I saw it all. I planned it all.

SANDY: You planned it all?

KING: Yes, I have been looking for someone in my land who thinks of others, someone willing to do things without the help of the king. I waited all day, and at last I found you.

SANDY: All day, sir! Why, anyone could move that stone.

KING: Anyone could do it, but only you did it. God bless you! The gold is yours.

STORYTELLER: What's the big idea?

If something needs to be done, do it yourself.

If it's right, do it.

The Tiger, the Brahman, and the Jackal

Characters

TIGER
BRAHMAN
TREE
WATER BUFFALO

ROAD
JACKAL
CAGE, three or more
actors

SCENE. *A clearing in a jungle in India. Tree stands left stage. Road is lying right stage. Tiger is center stage in a cage formed by three or more actors who join hands.*

TIGER: Help! Help! Let me out! I am dying of thirst. Help! (*Brahman enters*) Oh, Brahman, good, kind Brahman, please let me out. I am dying of thirst.

BRAHMAN: Let you out, Tiger? No, indeed! The first thing you would do is eat me up.

TIGER: Oh, no, kind sir. You misunderstood me. I would not eat you up.

BRAHMAN: What would you do?

TIGER: I would be your slave for life.

BRAHMAN: Sorry, A brahman doesn't need a slave.

TIGER: Please let me out. I'll go to the ends of the earth with you doing good deeds.

BRAHMAN: Sorry, Tiger, I plan to stay right here.

TIGER: Oh, Brahman, you live. I die of thirst. Is it just for one to live and another to die? Please, let me out! Please! Please! Please!

BRAHMAN: True, it is not just for one to live and another to die. (*goes to cage; opens door by taking hand of one actor who steps forward*) There, I'll let you out.

TIGER (*rushing out of cage*): Now, I'll eat you up!

BRAHMAN: (*running behind cage and peeking out*): No, Tiger! No! No! You promised not to eat me. You promised!

TIGER (*snarling and advancing slowly*): What's a promise in the jungle?

(*Brahman dashes behind tree and looks out.*)

BRAHMAN: Please, Tiger! Please! Ask three things in the jungle if it's fair.

TIGER: All right! Ask three things—the first three things you see. (*goes to side of cage; sits down*) I'll wait right here.

BRAHMAN: Well, Tree. (*comes to right of tree*) Tree, is it fair for Tiger to eat me? He was trapped. He pleaded for mercy. I freed him. Is it fair for him to eat me now?

TREE: Why should you complain? I give shelter to all who pass by. In return, they break my branches. Don't whimper. Take your medicine like a man.

BRAHMAN: Oh, dear!

TIGER (*smiling*): See?

(*Water Buffalo enters slowly right.*)

BRAHMAN: Oh, Water Buffalo. (*Water Buffalo walks past Brahman without looking at him or turning. Brahman follows him.*) Good, aged, sir. (*Water Buffalo turns.*) Tell me. Is it fair for Tiger to eat me? He was trapped. He pleaded for mercy. I let him out. Shouldn't he be grateful?

WATER BUFFALO (*turning slowly to look at Brahman*): Grateful? Who is grateful? When I was young, men gave me cotton seed and oil cakes. Now I am old, they put a yoke on me and feed me stale fodder. What can you expect? (*stands beside Tree*)

BRAHMAN: But, Water Buffalo—

(*Water Buffalo pays no attention.*)

TIGER (*smiling*): See?

BRAHMAN (*going to Road*): Oh, Road! (*Road sits up slowly, half interested.*) Road you saw and heard it all. Is it fair for Tiger to eat me?

ROAD: Here I am, useful to everyone—rich and poor, young and old, man and beast. What do men do for me? Litter me with everything they want to drop.

(*Jackal enters and interrupts.*)

JACKAL: Hey! What goes on here? (*Brahman faces Jackal.*) Oh, Brahman, you look like a fish out of water. What's the trouble?

BRAHMAN: Oh, Jackal, Tiger was trapped in a cage. He pleaded for mercy. I freed him. Now he

81

wants to eat me. Tree, Water Buffalo, and Road all say it's fair. Do you think it's fair for Tiger to eat me?

TIGER (*getting up*): Yes, it's fair. The law of the jungle. (*Starts toward Brahman. Jackal steps between Tiger and Brahman.*)

JACKAL: Wait a minute. It's all very confusing. Let's go to the cage. Explain again.

TIGER: Back where we started? Let's begin our dinner.

JACKAL: Our dinner—our dinner. I don't quite understand. My poor brain. Let me see how did this begin. (*to Brahman*) You were in the cage and Tiger came walking by.

TIGER: Pooh! What a fool you are! I was in the cage.

JACKAL (*pretending to be frightened*): Of course, I was in the cage. No, I wasn't. Let me see. The Tiger was in the Brahman. The cage came walking by—No, no! Dear, dear!

TIGER: Listen! I'll make you understand. See, I'm the Tiger.

JACKAL: Yes, you're the Tiger.

TIGER: That's the Brahman.

JACKAL: Yes, that's the Brahman.

TIGER: That's the cage.

JACKAL: Yes, that's the cage.

TIGER: I was in the cage. Do you understand?

JACKAL: Please, please! How did you get in?

TIGER: The usual way, of course.

JACKAL: I don't understand. Show me how you got in.

TIGER (*getting very angry*): How did I get in? Look, like this. (*steps into cage*) And then—

(*Jackal slams door shut, by quickly leading actor who is door back into circle. Actors in circle grasp hands firmly to indicate that the gate is locked tight.*)

JACKAL: And then you can stay there. (*to Brahman*) Come, Brahman, let us say good-bye to Tree. (*They bow to Tree. Tree returns bow.*) To Water Buffalo. (*They bow to Water Buffalo. Water Buffalo returns bow.*) To Road. (*They bow to Road. Road returns bow.*) To Cage. (*They bow to Cage. Cage returns bow.*) And to Tiger. (*They bow to Tiger.*)

TIGER: Grrrrrrrr!

(*Brahman and Jackal exit as Tiger continues to growl.*)

STORYTELLER: What's the big idea?

Beware of false promises.

Clever—Eh?

Characters

ANNETTE, a French
 refugee
PIERRE, her husband
HANS, a German
 woodcutter

FRAU SCHMIDT,
 innkeeper
GRETCHEN, serving
 maid
JACOB, kitchen boy

SCENE 1. *Along a road in Westphalia, Germany, 1794. Pierre and Annette are picking up a few sticks. They are very tired and cold. (This scene can be played in front of a curtain.)*

ANNETTE: Pierre, we'll never get enough wood this way.

PIERRE: What can we do? We can't go into the forest. Only a German can cut wood in the forest—a German with a permit.

ANNETTE: We'll never heat our hut.

PIERRE: We're lucky to have a hut.

ANNETTE: Lucky? We spent a lot to get our hut. Oh, why did we leave France?

PIERRE: Shhhhh—Annette! You know why we left France. You know we can't go back—at least not now. We must live as best we can on the little money we have left.

ANNETTE: How much money do we have?

PIERRE: Three gold louies. That's all we have. Three gold coins.

ANNETTE: Then let's buy wood. We can buy wood and have money left.

PIERRE: Where can I buy wood?

ANNETTE: Ask a German. Here comes someone. He looks German.

PIERRE: Can he understand my German?

ANNETTE: I think so. People understand us when we want to buy something.

(*Pierre approaches Hans as he enters.*)

HANS: Well, hello! What are you two people doing?

ANNETTE: Gathering sticks, as you can see.

HANS: What for?

ANNETTE: To heat our hut.

HANS: Heat a hut with sticks? How can you heat a hut with sticks?

ANNETTE: We can't. That's the problem.

PIERRE: We need wood. We must have wood. Do you know where we can get wood?

HANS: I know where you can *buy* wood. That's my job, selling wood. I'm a woodcutter.

ANNETTE: Will you sell us wood?

HANS: For a price.

PIERRE: What price?

HANS: Let me see your money before we bargain.

ANNETTE: Show him, Pierre. I'm very cold.

PIERRE: All right, Annette. (*takes a gold coin*

from his pocket) I have no change. Can you make change for this?

(*Pierre holds coin in his hand. Hans stares at it.*)

HANS: Change for a gold louie? You think you can buy wood and get change for a gold louie? Well, you are new around here. You haven't heard about inflation.

ANNETTE: Oh, please, sir! Please sell us a lot of wood for one gold louie. All we have left is three gold louies. Please sell us wood for one gold louie.

PIERRE: Certainly one gold louie is more than enough for a load of wood.

HANS: A cart of wood—three gold louies. Take it or leave it. (*no answer*) Do you freeze or do you live?

(*Annette and Pierre look at each other in despair. They are very cold. At last Pierre speaks.*)

PIERRE: Come to our hut. Let's talk where the wind blows less.

(*All exit.*)

SCENE 2. *Later that day at an inn in Westphalia. A table with two chairs at the back is set downstage center. Gretchen and Jacob are busy backstage cleaning. Frau Schmidt is polishing the table top. Hans enters in a jolly mood.*

FRAU SCHMIDT: Well hello, Hans! Take off your coat. Sit down.

HANS (*taking off coat and sitting down*): Thank you, I'll do just that.

FRAU SCHMIDT: What would you like today? Bean soup as usual?

HANS: Bean soup. Oh, no, not today. Frau Schmidt. Today I'll have hasenpfeffer, boiled cabbage, apple strudel, washed down with mugs of ale. In short, give me the best in the house!

FRAU SCHMIDT: Gretchen, Jacob, you heard Hans' order. Wait on him. (*She sits next to Hans.*)

FRAU SCHMIDT: Now, may I ask you, friend Hans, how do you plan to pay for all this?

HANS: With gold, Frau Schmidt, with gold.

FRAU SCHMIDT: How did you get your gold?

HANS: With head. Clever, eh? Call me Clever Hans.

FRAU SCHMIDT: How, clever Hans? Do tell me.

HANS: You'll never believe me.

(*Gretchen and Jacob enter with dishes of food. Stand holding them.*)

FRAU SCHMIDT: I don't believe you have gold. (*to Gretchen and Jacob*) Don't put a dish on this table until Clever Hans shows me his gold.

HANS: So you don't believe me. You don't think I'm clever. (*slams gold on table*) See!

FRAU SCHMIDT: I see. Gretchen, Jacob, set the table.

(*They do so.*)

HANS: This looks delicious.

(*He picks up his knife and fork. Frau Schmidt stops him from eating.*)

FRAU SCHMIDT: I'm sure it is. But before you eat, tell me, Clever Hans, how you got these coins. (*picks them up and examines them*) They're French coins.

HANS: Oh, yes, they are French coins. I can spot a Frenchman when I see him.

FRAU SCHMIDT: Or listen to him.

HANS: More to the point. Well, I'll tell you I was walking down the road, and I met two people, poor people, picking up sticks, little bits of sticks.

He says, "Do you know where I can get wood?"

Right away, I know he's French. Clever me. I've got good ears. (*Frau Schmidt nods.*) She called him "Pierre." He called her, "Annette."

Then I think, "They're refugees." (*Frau Schmidt nods.*) "Most refugees have some money, usually gold money." So I kept talking.

At last the woman said, "Three gold louies. That's all we have—three gold louies."

So I think, "They're cold. They're freezing. They need wood. What will they pay for a load? Three gold louies?"

"Three gold louies for a load of wood!" they scream.

"Inflation," I say. "Three gold louies for a load of wood. Pay me before I put a stick into your house."

Now, Frau Schmidt, do you understand what I mean, Clever Hans?

FRAU SCHMIDT: Oh, yes, I understand, Clever

Hans. (*rises*) Now pay me before you eat a bit of food.

HANS: Gladly. How much?

FRAU SCHMIDT: Three gold louies.

HANS (*rising*): Three gold louies for a meal! (*picks up coins*) That's cheating!

FRAU SCHMIDT: Or inflation. Three gold louies for a load of wood. Three gold louies for a meal. Clever, eh, Hans?

(*Hans turns to go.*)

FRAU SCHMIDT: Stop, Hans! Three gold louies or I call the police. Let a judge decide: "What is cheating? What is inflation?" Jacob, hold his horse and wagon until the police arrive. (*Jacob starts to go.*)

HANS: I need my horse and wagon.

FRAU SCHMIDT: After you give me three gold louies.

HANS (*changing tone of voice*): Oh, you can't fool Clever Hans. I'll tell the judge that you charged three gold louies for a simple meal.

FRAU SCHMIDT: All right. I'll return the coins to Pierre and Annette. They'll tell the judge the whole story.

(*Hans and Frau Schmidt glare at each other. At last Hans hands over the coins.*)

FRAU SCHMIDT: Thank you, Hans. Now eat the meal. You paid for it.

HANS: Never! (*stamps out of inn*)

FRAU SCHMIDT: Jacob, go find Pierre and Annette in their hut near the woods. Tell them I found three French coins. Ask them to be my guests for dinner. Or I should say, "the guests of Clever Hans"?

STORYTELLER: What's the big idea?

Cheating's not the same as being clever.

Who Would Steal a Penny?

Characters

MRS. NORA	JASON
ANDY NORA	JODIE
SARAH	TODD
PAM	OTHER CLUB MEMBERS

Parts may be played by either boys or girls. Do not crowd the stage or stage area with too many Club Members.

SCENE. *Meeting place of the Coin and Stamp Club. A coffee table is placed downstage center front. As the scene opens, Mrs. Nora and Andy are putting three chairs or low stools and some large cushions around the back and ends of the table. Phone rests on small table backstage. Sarah wears a dress or slacks with a pocket.*

MRS. NORA: Some people can sit on the floor.

ANDY: Why not? They always do.

MRS. NORA: Here they come.

(Andy goes to door. He and Mrs. Nora greet Club Members as they troop in and gather around back and ends of table. For a few seconds there is a babble of "Hi, Jason!" "Hi! Jodie!" "Hi, Todd!" and so on. Mrs. Nora sits on the center chair or stool. Pam and Sarah sit on the other two. Andy, Todd, Jodie, and Jason remain standing. Other Club Members sit down.)

MRS. NORA: Did anyone get an interesting coin this summer?

TODD: I'll say! Look at this one from Finland.

ANDY: Let's see. *(Todd shows coin.)* That's keen!

(Others look at coin with appropriate remarks. This dialogue must move fast.)

JODIE: Here's a Japanese coin.

TONY: This is from Italy.

(Again there is general interest. Andy exits and reenters with bowl of potato chips but doesn't put them on coffee table at once.)

PAM: I have a special American coin, an Indian head penny.

MRS. NORA: Really? I haven't seen an Indian head penny for ages! Let me see it.

(*Pam stands and gives Mrs. Nora the penny.*)

SARAH: Let me see it. (*She stands on the other side of Mrs. Nora and examines penny.*) Sure enough! An Indian head penny, 1903. My grandmother started a collection of Indian head pennies when she was my age.

JASON: She did? That's great. Let me see the penny.

(*Sarah hands penny to Jason.*)

MRS. NORA: You're lucky, Pam. I think Indian head pennies are getting rare.

TODD: I want to look at it.

OTHERS: Pass it around.

(*Andy sets bowl of potato chips in center of table as other Club Members pass coin to each other.*)

ANDY: Might as well eat as you look.

(*Members scoop up potato chips as they pass coin hastily from one person to another. Pam and Sarah only pretend to be eating.*)

MRS. NORA: Let's start the meeting. It's Jodie's turn to give a report.

PAM: Excuse me, Mrs. Nora. Who has my Indian head penny?

CLUB MEMBERS: Not me! Not me!

PAM: Someone must have it.

(*Club Members shake heads. Hold up empty hands.*)

PAM: Where is it?

MRS. NORA: Let's look.

(*Club members look under pillows, table, chairs. Mrs. Nora lifts dish. Gives up search.*)

MRS. NORA: Where can it be?

PAM: Someone stole my Indian head penny.

MRS. NORA: Why would anyone steal your penny?

PAM: I don't know. If it isn't here, someone has it.

MRS. NORA: I'll tell you what we'll do. Everyone, turn your backs to the table. (*They do so.*) Now, close your eyes. I'll close my eyes and count to ten. Will the person who has the penny please put it on the table. (*Mrs. Nora closes her eyes.*) One, two, three, four, five, six, seven, eight, nine, ten. Open your eyes and turn around. (*They do so.*)

PAM: Where is my Indian head penny?

MRS. NORA: Yes, where is the penny? (*no answer*)

PAM: We'll have to search everyone. Someone has my coin.

MRS. NORA: I hate to do this, but we must find the coin. Everyone, empty your pockets and put everything on the table.

(*Club Members do so.*)

MRS. NORA (*looking at table*): No coin.

(*Club members chatter, "Where could it be?" and so on.*)

MRS. NORA: Pam and I will have to search you.

(*Club Members stand as Mrs. Nora and Pam quickly frisk each member who then sits down. Only Sarah remains standing. Mrs. Nora comes to her. Sarah grasps her pocket with both hands.*)

SARAH: No, you can't search me!

MRS. NORA: Sarah, you must let me search you.

SARAH: No! No! No!

PAM (*coming close to Sarah*): You stole my Indian head penny!

SARAH: I did not steal your penny!

PAM: You did!

SARAH: I didn't!

PAM: Thief!

(*Mrs. Nora separates girls.*)

MRS. NORA: Sarah, if you won't let me search you, I'll have to call your parents.

SARAH: All right. But I'll call them. They'll come right over.

(*Sarah goes to phone at back of stage. Club Members are excited.*)

ANDY: Cool it! Cool it! I'll get more chips while she's calling. (*He stands in back of coffee table. Starts to pick up dish.*) Hey! Look! (*lifts coin out of dish*) Here's the Indian head penny. In the bottom of the dish. Someone dropped it while getting potato chips.

(*Pam comes downstage to Andy. He hands penny to Pam. Sarah comes downstage.*)

PAM: My penny! (*rushes to Sarah*) Sarah, I'm

sorry! I thought you stole my Indian head penny. (*hugs her*)

SARAH: I know.

(*Mrs. Nora stands next to Sarah.*)

MRS. NORA: We're all sorry. But, Sarah, why wouldn't you let me search you?

(*Sarah puts her hand into her pocket. Pulls out a coin.*)

SARAH: Because I have an Indian head penny just like Pam's. Grandma gave me one of hers.

MRS. NORA (*looking at coin*): An Indian head—1903.

SARAH: I didn't have a chance to show it.

STORYTELLER: What's the big idea?

Button your lip until you have all the facts.

Half of the Reward

Characters

STORYTELLER   FIRST SERVANT
MARIA, a peasant   SECOND SERVANT
IVAN, her husband   THIRD SERVANT
TZAR

PLAYS

SCENE 1. *A field worked by a Russian peasant. (This is played in front of the curtain.) Maria is hoeing as Storyteller gives background of the play.*

STORYTELLER: The scene is Old Russia at a time when peasants tilled the fields, cut wood, repaired roads, and did other hard work. These peasants had little to call their own. Only the Tzar and his nobles owned beautiful jewels and gold. Here we see Maria working. (*exits*)

(*Ivan enters running and calling excitedly.*)

IVAN: Maria! Maria! Look what I found. Look! (*shows her a stone*)

MARIA: Ivan, it's beautiful! I never saw such a beautiful stone.

IVAN: I'll make a necklace for you.

MARIA: Thank you, Ivan. I've never had a necklace with a pretty stone. (*She takes stone and looks at it more carefully.*) Ivan, maybe this isn't just a stone.

IVAN: What do you mean, "Just a stone"? It's a stone I found in the woods.

(*Maria scrubs stone with her skirt.*)

MARIA: Look. It's a cut stone.

IVAN: What's the difference? It's still a pretty stone.

MARIA: No, Ivan, it's a jewel.

IVAN: Good! I'll make a necklace with a jewel.

MARIA (*sadly*): No, Ivan, you can't.

IVAN: Why not?

97

MARIA: Because this jewel must belong to the Tzar. Only the Tzar or a nobleman would own a jewel like this.

(*Ivan pauses. He understands what Maria is going to say before she says it.*)

MARIA: You must take this jewel to the Tzar.

IVAN: Oh, Maria, I want to make a necklace for you—a necklace with a pretty stone.

MARIA: I know, and I thank you. But I could never enjoy a necklace with a stone that belongs to someone else.

IVAN: Why?

(*Maria looks him straight in the eye. She no longer speaks sweetly. She hands him the jewel. Puts her hands on her hips and speaks loudly and clearly.*)

MARIA: A spy would see the jewel and tell the Tzar I stole it. The Tzar would—

IVAN (*interrupting*): You are right, Maria. I must take the jewel to the Tzar. I must go at once. (*He ties the jewel in a handkerchief and clutches it tightly.*) Good-bye, Maria.

MARIA: Good-bye, Ivan, and good luck!

(*Maria turns. Wipes tears from her eyes. Throws back her shoulders and exits. Ivan walks across stage in opposite direction.*)

SCENE 2. *Entrance to palace. (This scene is also played in front of curtain, center.) First Servant stands at attention.*

STORYTELLER: After walking miles and miles, Ivan reaches the gate of the palace where he meets a servant of the Tzar. (*exits*)

(*Ivan walks until he reaches First Servant.*)

FIRST SERVANT: Halt!

(*Ivan stands stiff.*)

FIRST SERVANT: Who are you?

IVAN: Ivan, a peasant.

FIRST SERVANT: Obviously a peasant. What do you want?

IVAN: I wish to see the Tzar.

FIRST SERVANT: So you want to see the Tzar! What makes you think that the Tzar wants to see you?

IVAN: I have something to give him.

FIRST SERVANT: Give it to me, and I'll take it to the Tzar.

IVAN: No, sir, I must place this in the hands of the Tzar. I must do it myself.

FIRST SERVANT (*growing angry*): Listen! No one sees the Tzar unless I say he can see the Tzar. What do you want to give the Tzar?

IVAN: I think I found a crown jewel, sir.

FIRST SERVANT: Ah, then the Tzar will give you a reward.

IVAN: Oh—

FIRST SERVANT: I'll let you pass only on one condition.

IVAN: On what condition?

FIRST SERVANT: You must give me half of any reward that the Tzar gives you.

IVAN (*hesitating*): Well—well—

FIRST SERVANT: You can't see the Tzar unless you give me half of the reward.

IVAN (*still thinking*): I must see the Tzar. So—Well— All right. I'll give you half the reward if you let me see the Tzar.

FIRST SERVANT: This way.

(*First Servant leads the way offstage and Ivan follows.*)

SCENE 3. *Tzar is seated in a large chair, a servant on either side. First Servant and Ivan enter. Bow.*

TZAR: Speak.

FIRST SERVANT: Sir, this peasant says that he has found a precious jewel. I haven't seen it. But that's his story.

IVAN: It's a true story, sir. I found this stone in the woods. It's cut like a jewel. I thought it must belong to you.

(*Ivan hands jewel to Tzar who examines it carefully.*)

TZAR (*happily*): It is a jewel! The stone I lost—the stone I thought I'd never see again. Oh, peasant you shall have a reward. Name your reward.

IVAN: Fifty lashes, sir.

TZAR: Fifty lashes! Are you crazy?

IVAN: Not really, sir. Twenty-five of the lashes belong to this servant. (*points to First Servant, who cringes*)

TZAR (*roaring*): What!

IVAN: You see, your servant made me promise to give him half of any reward you gave me. He wouldn't let me in, unless I promised to give him half of my reward. So please give him twenty-five lashes.

TZAR (*laughing*): So! So! An honest peasant and a dishonest servant. (*to other servants*) Take this servant away and give him the total reward the peasant requested. Give him fifty lashes.

(*Second and Third Servants drag First Servant out of room.*)

TZAR: You, honest peasant, shall have a thousand rubles as a reward.

IVAN: Thank you, sir.

TZAR: And oh, yes, a gift in memory of today, something your family can always keep. What would you like?

IVAN: A necklace with a pretty stone to give my wife, Maria.

TZAR: It's yours, honest—and may I add, crafty—peasant.

STORYTELLER: What's the big idea?

Sometimes you get what's coming to you.

Honesty is the best policy.

Appendixes

Directions for Making
Simple Puppets

Puppet Construction

When you go to a puppet show, you watch the puppets and listen to the puppeteer who acts like one character. Both the puppets and the puppeteer are important as attention-getters. The voice of the puppeteer has a quality and variety that makes you want to listen. The appearance of the puppets makes you want to watch. As a rule, their looks are somewhat unusual and movements are exaggerated.

When you make a puppet, you can be as creative as you wish. You can use all kinds of materials and a combination of colors that will attract attention.

When putting on a play from this book, you can use bought puppets if you have some. Slip new dresses over their smocks if you want to change characters. Or make puppets.

The puppets described here are easy and inexpensive to make. Select the kind best suited to the skit or play you have chosen. Also consider the audience. If you are giving a play for friends, family, or classmates seated in a fairly small room, you can use little or large puppets. If you are giving a puppet play for an entire Cub pack, seated in an auditorium, you'll need bigger puppets that can be seen at a distance.

APPENDIXES

Stick Puppet

Materials. Lightweight cardboard (such as cereal box), construction paper, schoolroom glue or paste, crayons or paints.

Equipment. Scissors.

A stick puppet is really a paper doll glued or pasted onto the top part of a strip of cardboard or heavy paper. The puppeteer holds onto the lower end of the stick as he manipulates the puppet.

Cut a strip of lightweight cardboard or heavy paper one inch wide and about eleven inches long.

Decide if the puppet to be used in the skit should appear in profile or full face. On construction paper, draw a picture of the character about seven inches high. Cut it out and color face, clothing, fur, or whatever the character needs.

If the character drawn in profile must turn around in the play, make two identical pictures. If a full-faced puppet must turn around, draw a rear-view as well as a front view of the figure. Glue the cardboard stick between matching shapes.

Bag-head Puppet

Materials. Paper bag, newspaper, string, a lath or other sturdy stick, paints, construction paper, glue, staples.

Equipment. Paintbrush.

Only the head of a bag-head puppet shows above

a barrier during a puppet play. To make one, stuff a paper bag loosely with newspaper. Leave room at the bottom for tying.

Put a sturdy stick, about a foot longer than the bag, well into the bag. Rearrange the newspaper if necessary.

Tie the bottom of the bag around the stick.

Paint features of the face. If the puppet is an animal that needs whiskers, cut some of construction paper and glue in place. If the puppet needs ears, cut some out of brown bag paper and staple in place.

If the puppet is a human, put a cap or hat on its head or paint the bag to resemble hair. Or cut wide strips of construction paper and glue or staple in place for strands of hair.

Mitt Puppet

Materials. Scrap cloth, thread, scrap paper, carbon paper, pencil, crayons, or magic markers.

Equipment. Scissors, pins, needle.

Draw on a piece of scrap paper the outline of a mitten larger than your hand. Draw a pinky finger as well as a thumb on the outline. Draw the face of an animal or person on the center part of the mitt.

Using carbon paper, trace the face and outline onto a piece of cloth. Color the face with crayons or magic markers. (If you want to use paints, first

CUT ALONG

experiment on a scrap of cloth to see if colors tend to spread.)

Lay the cloth face and outline on another piece of cloth. Pin the two pieces together. Cut out around the outline of the mitt. Sew the two pieces of cloth together around the edges of the mitt, leaving the part for the wrist open.

Put on the mitt and use it as a hand puppet.

Wadded-paper Puppet

Material. Paper, string, paste, paint, cardboard tube or lightweight cardboard, gummed tape, paper toweling.

Equipment. Scissors, paintbrush.

Cut a cardboard tube a little longer than your index finger. If you do not have a tube, make one of lightweight cardboard, such as a cereal box. Roll the cardboard so that it fits easily over your index finger. Fasten the loose edge with gummed tape.

Crumple newspaper and shape it around the tube until you have the shape of a head. Cover all the tube except a little at the lower end. Wind string around the wad until the paper stays in place. Tear pieces of paper toweling into pieces roughly two inches square. Paste them onto the wad, overlapping the edges until the newspaper is covered. Fill in any dents with small wads of newspaper and cover with pasted toweling.

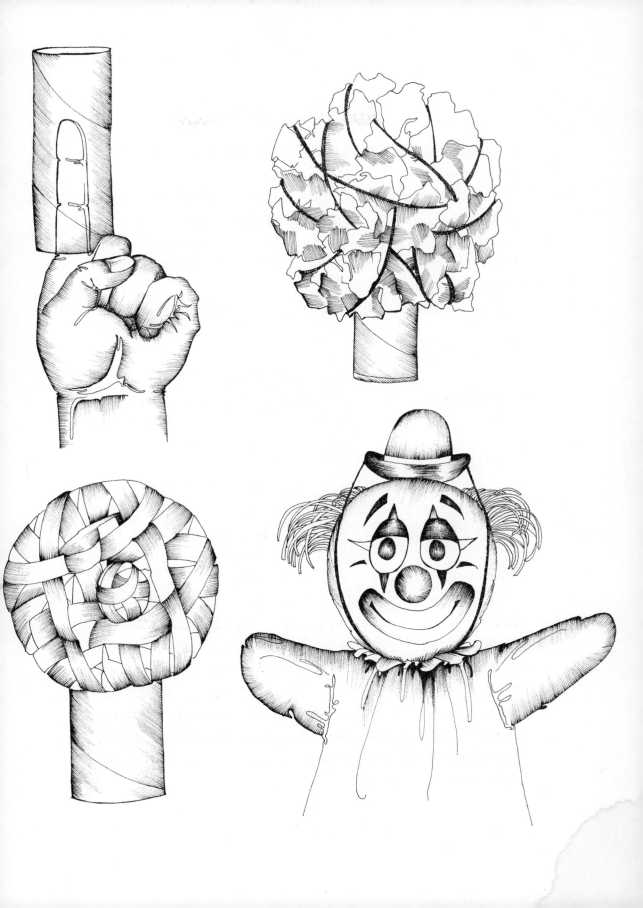

If you want to make a snout or protruding lips and jaw (for example, a monkey face) wad newspaper into shape, paste in place, and cover with small squares of toweling. Make ears the same way.

Allow the head to dry for a few days, and then paint it.

Drape a big handkerchief or other kind of cloth over your hand and wrist. Place the puppet head on your draped index finger. Extend your thumb and pinky fingers for arms. Wiggle the fingers under the cloth as the puppet talks. (If the head of an animal should come off in a skit, give your finger a flip to get the result you want.)

Clay-head Puppet

Materials. Plasticine, other kind of clay, or play dough, paints; popsicle stick or other stick; bits of straw if needed for whiskers; dinner-sized paper napkin or square of cloth that size; two rubber bands.

Equipment. Paintbrush, bottle or can in which to place puppet.

Roll some plasticine or other clay into a ball. Squeeze it, pinch it, and mold it into the shape of a head. If you want to add ears or the snout of an animal, model them of small pieces of clay. Put them on the face and smooth the clay.

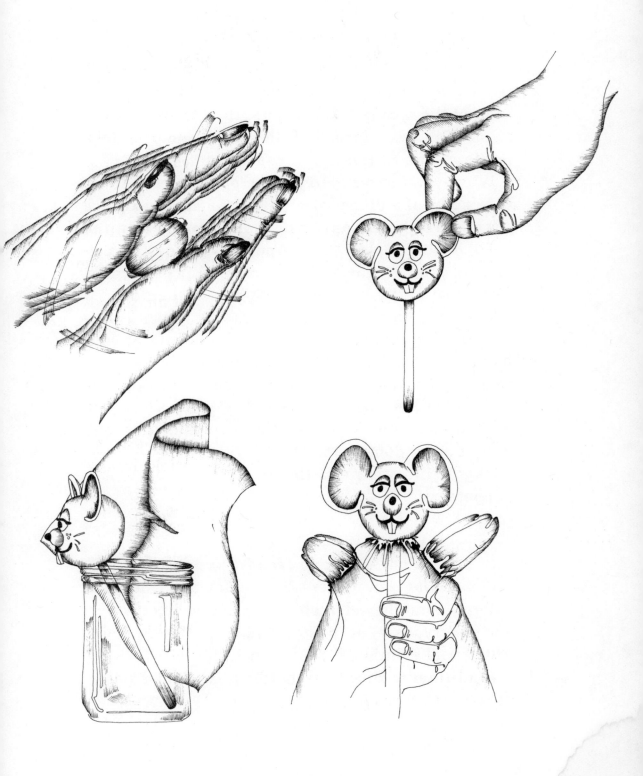

Press a popsicle stick or other stick into the clay, leaving a handle.

Paint the face if the clay is not the color you want. Paint features. Place the stick of the puppet in a bottle or can to hold the head upright

When you are ready to use the puppet, cut a slit in the center of a dinner-sized paper napkin or a piece of scrap cloth the same size. Don't worry about the color of the napkin. In the puppet world of make-believe you can have a blue elephant or green cow. The color of the head need not match the body.

Put the puppet stick through the hole in the napkin. Grasp it with the last three fingers of your hand under the paper or cloth. To make arms, extend your thumb and pointer finger in opposite directions. Put one rubber band over the cloth and around your thumb and another over the cloth and around your pointer finger.

Wiggle the stick and the arms as you become a puppeteer.

Papier-mâché Head Puppet

Materials. Newspaper—both black and white and colored comic sheets; white paper toweling; water; wallpaper paste or paste made by mixing flour, water, and a little salt; plasticine; paints.

Equipment. Bowls for holding water and paste, pencil, paintbrush.

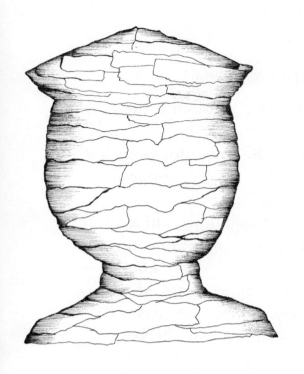 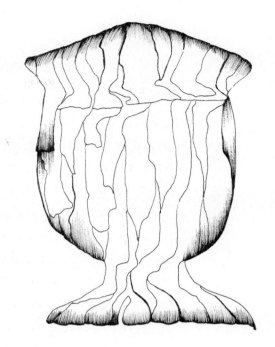

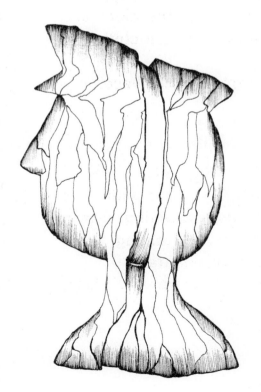 

Model a puppet's head with plasticine, making sure to include the shoulders. They help hold on the puppet's dress and allow the head to stand upright while drying.

Make the eyes and mouth large and deep; the cheeks very full, or sunken according to the needs of the character; and the nose, or in the case of an animal, the snout, big.

Tear sheets of newspaper, both black and white and colored, into bits about one-half inch wide and two inches long. Torn strips are better than cut because rough edges overlap.

Dip black and white strips into water and stick them onto the plasticine horizontally (crossways) overlapping the edges. When the head is covered, press paper to make indentations for eyes and mouth. Using a pencil may help. Smooth the paper.

Dip strips of colored newspaper into the paste. Stick them onto the head vertically (up and down). If small areas of black and white paper show, tear bits of paper and paste them in place, making the surface smooth. Again press paper to make indentations.

Add a third layer of papier-mâché, pasting black and white strips horizontally.

For the fourth and last layer, paste strips of white paper toweling diagonally. Again press indentations.

Set the head aside to dry for several days.

When it is thoroughly dry, take a paring knife and carefully cut through the papier-mâché from the side of a shoulder, up over the head and down to the edge of the other shoulder. Gently pull the two sides of papier-mâché apart. Take out the plasticine.

Tear paper toweling into strips about two inches long.

Fit together the two sides of the head. Paste strips of paper toweling across the crack, thus holding the parts of the head together.

Cover the entire head with paste-covered toweling going diagonally. Toweling will stretch a little, making it easy to cover curved areas and keep them smooth. Using a pencil, press eyes and mouth and any desired creases.

If you want the puppet to have eyebrows, dip strips of paper into paste. Crumple them into a wad. Mold two wads into eyebrows. Press them onto the head and cover with small bits of paste-covered toweling to help them stay in place.

If the puppet needs ears, draw a pattern, allowing an inch tab at the straight edge. Cut four ears out of toweling.

To make an ear, paste two paper ears together, leaving the tab at the base unpasted. Shape it. Make another ear.

Separate the tabs on each ear and paste them into place on the head. Paste additional paper toweling over the tabs to hold ears in place. Set the puppet head aside to dry.

Paint the head the basic color of the puppet. Let the paint dry. Later paint features. If the puppet needs whiskers, glue heavy thread, pieces of straw, or pipestem cleaners in place. If the puppet needs hair or a mane, glue yarn, strips of crepe paper, or other material in place.

Puppet Dress

Materials. Scrap paper or part of a paper bag, cloth for smock of a person or skin of an animal, thread, crayons.

Equipment. Scissors, pencil, pins, needle.

A hand puppet, whether a person or an animal, wears a loose-fitting kimono-type dress that covers the hand and wrist of the puppeteer.

To make a pattern, fold a piece of scrap paper or part of a paper bag in half so that the fold will lie on the shoulders.

Lay the puppet head on the fold. Draw a dress with the waist 5½ inches wide, arms 3 inches long, and 2 inches wide, and skirt longer than the distance from the tip of your fingers to your wrist, about 8 inches.

Cut out the pattern. Fold it in half up and down. If the two sides aren't alike, trim to make them so.

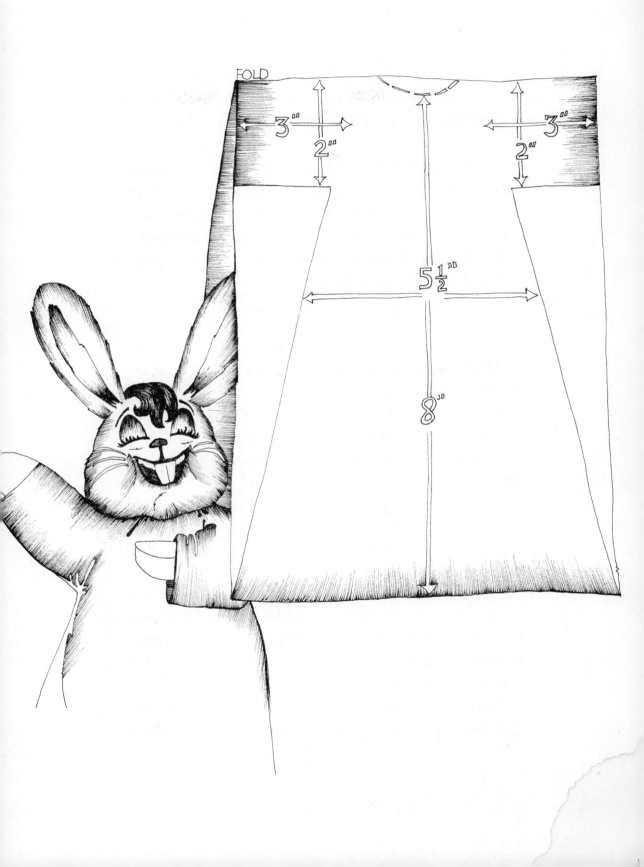

Cut a hole for the neck where the two folds meet. Slip the paper dress over the puppet head. If it doesn't fit, adjust it.

Fold the cloth for the dress in half. Pin the pattern on the cloth so that the shoulders are on the fold. Cut out the dress. If you are making an animal with spots or strips, color the dress with wax crayons.

If you want decorations on a dress of a human puppet, color the cloth with wax crayons or glue pieces of braid or patches of contrasting material.

Put the right sides of the dress together and sew the two sides. Turn the dress right side out. Sew around the neck with a running stitch, leaving the ends of the thread loose.

Put the dress or body of the animal over the puppet head and onto the shoulders. Pull the stitching tightly around the neck and tie the ends of thread together.

To operate the puppet, slip it over your hand with your index finger in the hollow head and your thumb and middle finger in the arms.

Stuffed-head Puppets

Materials. Cloth (for puppet head and for smock); thread; light-weight cardboard, such as cereal box, or heavy paper; colored ballpoint pens, cotton or cut-up pieces of old nylon stockings; gummed tape; pencil, carbon paper.

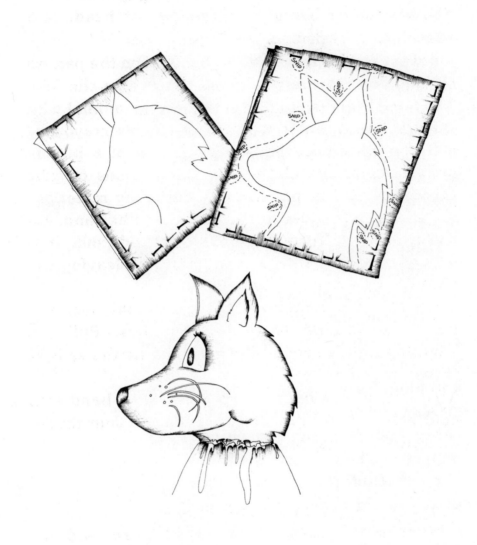

Equipment. Scissors, sewing machine.

Draw the profile of a character in a play: an animal, bird, or person, making the head as large as you want the puppet head to be. The neck must be 1½ inches across and 2 inches long.

Using carbon paper, trace the profile onto a piece of cloth. Pin another piece of cloth onto the back of the first piece. Do *not* cut the fabric at this time. It is easier to sew pieces of material together in a design before you cut them out than to sew small pre-cut pieces together.

Using a sewing machine, stitch on the outline through the two pieces of cloth, except across the bottom neck edge. Leaving a ¼-inch margin around the outline, cut out the figure. Where there is a curve in the design, snip very carefully from the outside of the cloth to the stitching. Do not cut the stitching. Turn the figure right side out.

Draw eyes, nose, and mouth on the figure with colored ballpoint pens or with something else. If the puppet needs ears, cut them out of scraps and sew in place. Stuff the nose with bits of cotton or cut-up pieces of old nylon stocking.

Roll a piece of lightweight cardboard or heavy paper into a tube as long or a little longer than your index finger and large enough around to fit over your index finger easily. Tape the edge of the tube in place. Insert the tube part way into the head of the puppet. Stuff cotton or cut-up pieces of old nylon stocking between the tube and the cloth head.

Make a kimono-type smock for the puppet, leaving the neck of the smock open. Insert the head of the puppet into the neck of the smock. Sew the head onto the smock.

Puppet Stage

To make a puppet stage, cut a large hole in the side of a cardboard carton. A large box, such as a refrigerator carton is best because you can stand up, hold the puppets over your heads, and speak so that everyone can hear you. It is easier to breathe deeply when you are standing than when you are in a stooped position.

If it is not practical to use a large box, you can make a stage from a smaller carton, the wider the better. Remove the top flaps. Turn the carton upside down. Cut out one long side, leaving a two-inch margin. This is the front of the stage.

Set up two card tables with a space between them. Drape an old sheet over the front of the tables. Rest the puppet stage on the tables. Adjust the vacant space between them so that you can kneel behind the sheet, reach up into the stage, and make your puppets act.

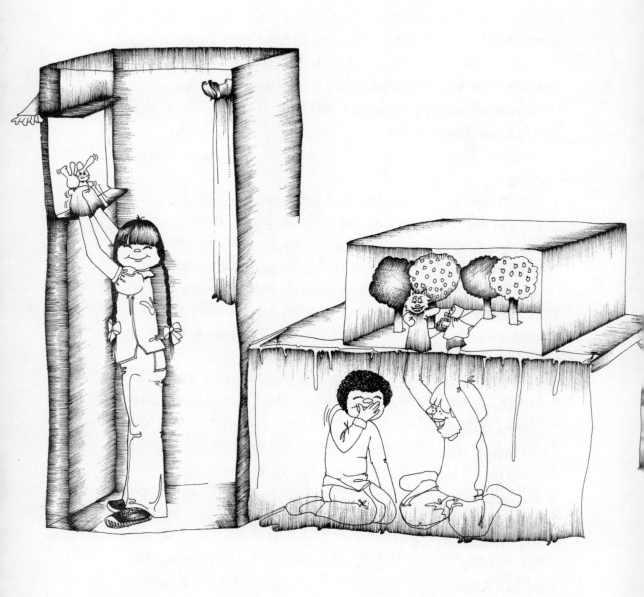

Glossary
of Stage Terms

Ad-lib: To make up lines or add words on the spur of the moment.

Bit player: Actor who plays a very small role.

Climax: Highest point of dramatic tension in a play.

Cue: A speech or action in a play that serves as a signal for another actor to speak or act.

Dialogue: Conversation in a play.

Downstage: The part of the stage nearest the audience.

Key lines: Lines that must be emphasized if the audience is to follow the plot or understand the message or joke of a play.

Lead: Most important character in a play.

Left stage: The part of the stage on the actors' left when they are facing the audience.

Offstage: Behind the scenes.

Onstage: The areas which the audience sees.

Pantomime: The art of acting silently, portraying a situation or an attitude with body movements or facial expressions but no sound.

Plot: Story and action of a play.

Props: Shortened term for "properties," any moveable object necessary to the action of a play.

Punch line: The line in a play that makes the point of the joke or message.

Puppeteer: One who manipulates or handles puppets in a show.

Right stage: The part of the stage on the actors' right when they are facing the audience.

Script: The written or printed play.

Supporting cast: Players who play important but not leading roles.

Index